SCHOOLBOY CRICKET:
The Boys' and Masters' Guide

SCHOOLBOY CRICKET:
The Boys' and Masters' Guide

by
RAYLEIGH G. STRUTT

*With 17 Illustrations
and 15 Diagrams*

Second Impression

HUTCHINSON'S
LIBRARY OF SPORTS AND PASTIMES
London   New York   Melbourne   Sydney   Cape Town

Printed in Great Britain
by The Anchor Press, Ltd.,
Tiptree, Essex

CONTENTS

PART I

LIST OF ILLUSTRATIONS

LIST OF ILLUSTRATIONS

*(All the instructional pictures were taken by Photo Finishers
(Sheffield) Ltd., and the diagrams drawn by Mr. Martin
Davenport, Sheffield.)*

PREFACE

My acknowledgments are due, and gratefully rendered, to Mr. J. le Pine Haigh, my successor as Headmaster of Westbourne Preparatory School, Sheffield, who first suggested that I should write this book. Subsequently he read the typescript and made several valuable suggestions.

To the Rev. Wm. Sawkins and Mr. F. K. Gardiner I express my thanks for their help and wise advice in the preparation of the book for publication.

I feel that I owe a profound debt to Mr. A. G. Marshall, Second Master (formerly Games Master) of Taunton School, under whose captaincy I played for fifteen years. From him, and from his brother, Dr. L. P. Marshall, I gathered the greater part of such cricket knowledge as I possess, and it is this knowledge, as it applies to schoolboys, that I attempt to pass on through the medium of this small work.

Finally, I express my great appreciation of Mr. Norman Yardley's kindness in writing the Foreword. Westbourne is a Yorkshire school and I am sure that all the boys will join with me in wishing Mr. Yardley and the Yorkshire XI the grandest possible season.

R. G. STRUTT.

Agden Lodge,
  Bradfield,
    Sheffield.

ACKNOWLEDGMENT

My best thanks are given to Duncan Gardiner,
Tony Trott and Andrew Jollie, who posed for
the photographs on a cold snowy day.

FOREWORD

I have read this little book with great interest and heartily commend it to would-be young cricketers and to those masters who have the all-important task of coaching young boys of preparatory school age.

It is a well-balanced book covering both the technical and practical problems of the game. I was particularly pleased to see that the author stresses the duties of Captaincy and Team Selection. These two subjects are just as important as Batting, Bowling and Fielding and require equally as much practice and experience.

The student is given food for thought on every page. His problems are simply and clearly explained, and any reader who absorbs this good common sense will indeed be the complete young cricketer.

Fortunately man is human and not a machine, hence all cricketers have their own methods, own strengths and weaknesses. Having grasped the basic principles or foundations it is then a matter of practice, experience and sensible application of one's own particular skill in the case of the pupil, and development and encouragement by the master. Genius and natural ability must be developed not ruined by text book teachings.

Schoolboy Cricket: The Boys' and Masters' Guide is a greatly needed addition to cricket literature and should be the guide and philosopher of every young cricketer and his coach.

NORMAN YARDLEY

11

Part I

TO BOYS AND THEIR MASTERS

CHAPTER I

YOU are keen! You would not be reading this unless you were. I want you to *remain* keen on this most glorious game, and in order to remain keen you must have some success. A few exceptional people are keen all their lives in spite of being "rabbits", but many boys when going on to their Public Schools or Grammar Schools find themselves in the lower games, where the standard of play and interest is poor. Their own interest evaporates and there's the end of it.

How very different is the case of the boy who leaves his Prep. School with a reputation and finds himself in the Colts or 2nd XI or even 1st XI his first Summer term! Such cases are rare, but most of you can aspire to the thrill of playing in your House 1st or 2nd XI immediately.

In what way can you attain to this reasonable success? By building solid foundations for your cricket. Nobody wishes all cricketers to be alike or all houses to be alike, but however different the final appearances of houses may be, they must all be built upon good concrete foundations. So with cricket. What are these foundations?

Before reading further: If you are a left-hander, get a pencil and look for the words "left-hand" in the rest of this chapter. Draw a line through and put "right-hand" instead. Then do the same with "left-leg", "left-shoulder", etc. This is far better than just saying to yourself, "Oh, I will change them round in my head as I read".

BATTING FOUNDATIONS

(1) The Right Sized Bat

It is tremendously important that the bat should not be too big or too heavy. It does not matter nearly so much if it is too small. Big, heavy bats have ruined the whole cricketing life of many people. If your father wants to buy you a good bat which will last you several years, make sure that it is the right size *at the beginning* and not of a size for you to grow up to.

Most schools now provide good bats of all sizes for the use of the boys, and it is far better to use the right school bat than to play with the wrong private one.

Your master will advise you, but a rough and ready test is this: If you stand upright, with your bat held straight up by your leg (the bottom on the ground), the top of the handle should not come quite as high as the bottom of your trouser pocket opening.

(2) Holding the Bat—Left Hand

Hold the bat firmly, in left hand only, nearly at the top, with the BACK OF THE HAND facing between "extra cover" and "mid-off". (See Plate I.) Now try this experiment:

Stand as if batting, and with the left elbow well up and holding the bat as above, and allowing the left wrist to bend naturally, swing the bat to and fro. Do you notice that it swings in an upright position; i.e. it is a "straight bat"? That is *correct*. Now start again and do everything the same except—have the back of the hand facing the imaginary bowler. Notice three things: (*a*) the bottom of the bat tends to stick away from you (crooked bat); (*b*) you do not feel so powerful; (*c*) the wrist tends to hinge in a way to spoon up a catch. That is wrong. Now do the same experiment with the back of the hand facing the wicket-keeper. This time the bat may be straight, and you may feel powerful, but you will feel rather stiff and awkward. It is wrong. Now return to the first part of the experiment so that you finish with the right feeling.

Holding the Bat—Right Hand

This should be near the left hand. It is tempting to have the hands apart, but the temptation must be resisted if you wish to develop free and flowing shots. It is very important that you should *not* grip the handle firmly in the right palm. Try this experiment to see why. Stand in the batting position and take hold of the bat firmly in the right palm, leave go with the left hand and try the backwards and forwards swing of the bat as you did in the left-hand experiment. Do you not find it impossible to swing with an upright (straight) bat? That must be wrong. The right hand should not be a GRIPPER but a PUSHER. Now hold the bat with the thumb and first finger of the right hand only. It will hang down in an upright position. Then let the other fingers close on to the handle. You can now *swing* the bat in an upright position. Add the left hand in its correct position and you are all set to make good strokes. Do not forget that the left-hand grip should be firm but the right-hand looser.

(I know that Herbert Sutcliffe holds the opposite view but he is a magnificent exception.)

Now before we go on to the third and fourth foundations, let me give your mind a little rest and tell you something which requires less concentration on your part. I refer to the way you stand at the wicket—stance. You should have the left shoulder pointing at the opposite wicket, both eyes looking at the bowler, and your feet should be *slightly* apart, the right foot just inside the crease. Some boys are so frightened of being stumped that they have both feet in. This is silly, because it makes it so much farther to reach the ball when cracking a half-volley or playing forward, and it also does not give you so much room to move back without treading on your wicket (out!).

Perhaps the most important thing is to have your weight equally on both feet so that you can move back (towards your stumps, *not* towards the square-leg umpire!) or forward most quickly. If your weight is chiefly on the left foot and you wish to put your left leg down the wicket, you have first to move the weight on to the right foot. This takes *time*—and you have not much time to spare!

Do you realize that it takes only about *half a second* for a ball to travel from a very fast bowler's hand to your wicket? You have not even that half-second in which to make your stroke, because you must wait to judge the length and direction of the ball! But do not feel discouraged. It is almost miraculous what trained muscles *with a properly developed muscular memory* can do in that very short time. Later in this book you will be told when and how to develop this wonderful muscular memory.

(3) Raising the Bat

It will probably surprise you to know that D. R. Jardine, the former England captain, is of the opinion that not one batsman in ten lifts his bat really correctly. And he was thinking about Test and County players! The remaining nine out of ten lift the bat so that it points towards the slips or even third man. How very much more difficult to bring it down the line of the ball! I will explain what I mean by this later on, but Mr. Jardine rightly asks why you should not be proud of doing at any rate one thing better than most of the famous players! I am now going to tell you of a safe way of lifting the bat correctly and a method of testing yourself.

PLATE 1. Swinging the straight bat with the left hand only. The bat is truly upright, though the angle from which the photo was taken makes it appear otherwise.

PLATE 2. Raising the bat. This is a good position. Notice the left wrist and how the left hand is, obviously, the master hand. The hands could well have been a little nearer the top end of the handle. Compare with Plate 5.

Take up the stance and grip, as you were told in the previous section. Now, without straightening your body, and with left elbow pointing at bowler, just bend both elbows, right elbow moving round to point at square-leg, and at the same time, rotate your left hand as if you were winding up a clock. If you are gripping firmly with your left hand, and mainly with thumb and first finger of right hand, your bat cannot help being in the right position. It will be pointing towards the middle or middle and leg stump and its *face* will be towards point, not towards the ground. Study Plate II carefully. It is very important.

The turning of the face of the bat towards point makes sure that your wrists come in to your shot; and this adds greatly to the "snap" and speed with which the ball travels.

Very many players make things much harder for themselves by standing at the wicket with their bats sloping at an angle, edge towards the bowler, hands resting on thighs, often with the right knee behind the bat. (See Plate III.)

Very comfortable, no doubt, and if comfort is the chief thing, just carry on. I would only suggest that if you took out a deck-chair with you, you would be still more comfortable. NO! Comfort is not the chief thing, but it is very important, and you can be perfectly comfortable with a more sensible stance. Now look at this photograph of the comfortable fellow, and think of all the movements he must make before he can get his bat up correctly. (1) He must get his right knee out of the way. (2) He must get his bat into an upright position. (3) He must turn the face of it towards the bowler. (4) He must bend his elbows and turn his left wrist as I have told you above.

If you have taken up a position like the one shown in Plate IV you can be perfectly comfortable, and yet you do not have to do movements 1, 2 and 3, but start straight

B

away with No. 4. Of course, what happens to people who stand as in Plate III is that they also leave out movements 1, 2 and 3; but they do not do 4 at all. They, too, make only one movement—the easy and natural one. They pull up with their right hands with the result shown in Plate V.

Do you see that if they now get a straight ball, the bat will either have to play across the flight of the ball or else describe an arc of a quarter of a circle before it can get on to the line?

Oh, why do people make it so hard for themselves? Batting against good bowling is difficult enough anyway, so why *add* difficulties? I have said a good deal, and given you several illustrations about this one point, because it is so very important and is a FOUNDATION.

Now for a test. Get a bat and stand facing a wall and close to it, so that when you bend forward into the correct batting position your head will be just touching the wall. The bottom of your bat will be a few inches from the wall. Now raise your bat in the correct way as described above, hold it there and have a look at it. You will see that its length is parallel to the wall and the face is parallel to the face of the wall. It is a perfect position. Your head is still just touching the wall too, and that is important, because many boys tend to straighten their bodies when they lift their bats. That is a bad fault because (*a*) you move your head and the head (really the eyes) should be as still as possible, (*b*) you cannot play with a straight (upright) bat, (*c*) you cannot get "over" the ball.

Having done this experiment you may care to take up the "comfortable" position shown in Plate III, by the wall. Now try to raise your bat, but don't blame me if you damage the back of it! Do you see that it is impossible to raise it correctly? From that moment never again take up that position except to show a friend how bad it is.

The mention of the friend gives me an opportunity to give your concentration another rest before going on to Foundation 4. Your Cricket Master will help you all he can, and in Part II of this book there are suggestions for valuable Winter work, but obviously, he cannot give you, personally, very much time, as he has so many other boys to help. You can do a good deal for yourself if you carefully study this book, and afterwards, some of the many splendid books by great cricketers; but a much better way is to join forces with a keen friend and *teach each other* cricket. This has several advantages; for the best way of learning a subject is to teach it, and you can see your friend's position better than he can himself, and *vice versa*. Also, your keenness and your friend's keenness more than add up—they multiply. If you think in terms of Algebra and let k stand for keenness, it is not $2k$ but k^2.

I remember that when I was a Preparatory Schoolboy I used to go to stay at Chelmsford with Gilbert Dixon, who afterwards played for Essex. We had a net in a field, and we generally got up at about six in the morning and had an hour and a half before breakfast practising cricket. From after breakfast until lunch we spent the time at the net. In the afternoon we sometimes had a bathe or played tennis, but we generally practised cricket; and, of course, after tea was a splendid opportunity of going to the net! Perhaps that was slightly overdoing it; and if we had spent less time, but on a definite plan, such as is suggested in this book, we should have had better results. We certainly got plenty of practice in hitting a moving ball (and fetching it), but you can imagine that by 6.30 p.m. the bowling was less hostile than it was at 6.30 a.m.

When I was at my Public School, my friend L. P. Marshall (who with his brother A. G. played for Somerset while they were still schoolboys) came to stay with us; and we put in nearly as much time at cricket as Gilbert

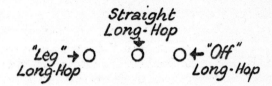

Straight
Long-Hop

"Leg" →   ○   ○   ○ ← "Off"
Long-Hop   Long-Hop

{
"Good Length"
Balls Pitch in
This Area
According To
Circumstances
}

Straight Half Volley
↓

Half-Volley → ○   ○   ○   Half-Volley
on "Leg"   On "Off"

✕   ○ ←
BATSMAN   "Yorker"

● ● ●

Some Types Of Ball.
The circles show where they pitch.

DIAGRAM A

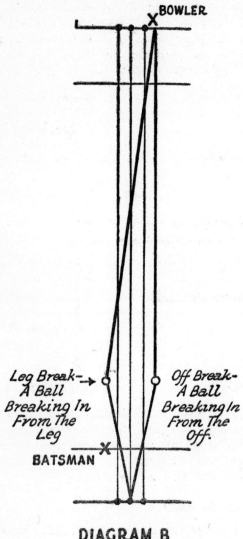

DIAGRAM B

Dixon and I used to do, though we did not start before breakfast. We had another great improvement, because by that time I had a young brother, aged six, to chase the balls for us. He spent the day doing this, and in the evening, we graciously allowed him a few minutes batting.

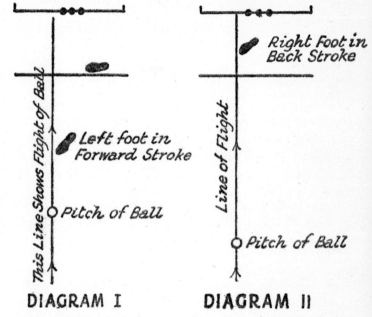

DIAGRAM I   DIAGRAM II

The small brother, C. W. Strutt, afterwards developed into an exceptionally good fielder and thrower (as well as being a fine batsman) so we may really have been doing him a good turn. Anyway, I think he enjoyed it. (See Diagrams A and B on pp. 20 and 21.)

(4) Placing the Feet

For all straight or nearly straight balls the left foot, when playing forward, or the right foot, when playing back, should be only just to the leg side of the line of the ball's flight. (See Diagrams I and II on p. 22).

This means that you can get your eyes in such a position that they are looking down the line of the ball; and also there will not be a gap between the bat and the leg. If there is a gap and the ball breaks from the off, it may use that gap to bowl you. You may say "Ah, but what about l.b.w.?" I reply that the nearer your leg is to the line of flight the *less* likely you are to be l.b.w.

To understand this you must be quite clear about the rule which (for balls pitching in a line between the two wickets or *to the off* of such a line) is this: If the Umpire thinks that the ball (1) pitched on the wicket or to the off-side, (2) would have hit the wicket, (3) was prevented from doing so by hitting some part of the batsman (except his hand), (4) *that part of the batsman was between the two wickets at the time it was hit*—then the decision is OUT.

Now look at the two diagrams on page 24.

They illustrate the same ball. The batsman's pad above his foot stops the ball in each case, but he is not out in the second case because his pad was outside of the line between the wickets. That is why I say you are less likely to be l.b.w. if your leg is close to the line of the ball.

It is not difficult to do this for over-pitched or short balls. In the first case you simply aim your left toe to a spot just beside that upon which the ball will pitch. The ball is a half-volley. You bang it to the boundary. In the case of a short ball, you move your weight across until your eyes are looking down the line of flight, plant down your right foot *with all your weight on it and a straight knee* and you will find it is automatically in the right place. But be sure to keep your head leading—that is to say, nearer the bowler than your right leg. This means it does not bob up and down. So far it is easy; but those are not

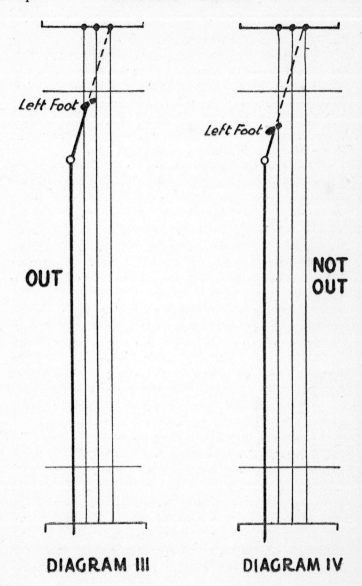

DIAGRAM III   DIAGRAM IV

the balls that would be likely to get you out anyway. It is the good length balls pitching between those two spots which get you out, and often it is by the ball finding the gap between bat and leg.

Do you know that after very many years of cricket it was only a few years ago that I discovered what I think to be the reason, and I have not seen it mentioned in other books on cricket, and I certainly was never told it by any of my coaches.

Down comes the ball on a line outside the off-stump. It is not pitched up near enough to you to be driven on the half-volley (i.e. just after it has pitched). You decide to play a forward defensive stroke, which means you (intend to) put your leg to the line of the ball and play it with an upright bat when the ball has reached the level of your leg—*and head*—for you are leaning forward and your head is over your bent left knee. Instead of the comforting feeling and sound of the meeting of bat and ball there is a sickening clatter behind you and revolting voices exclaim, "Oh, well bowled, sir!" if it was an off-break or —"well caught!" (in the slips) if it wasn't. You return to the pavilion disappointed and puzzled. You aimed your leg at the ball, didn't you? Yes! You played with a straight bat, didn't you? Yes! I think the diagrams on page 26 will help you to understand the explanation and help you to remedy the fault.

Diagram V illustrates how you played the ball. *You pointed your left foot at the spot where you thought the ball would pitch.* I have questioned many cricketers, and they all have told me that that is what they do. That is what I have done until lately—but think what it means. It means your eyes were not looking down the line of the flight of the ball. If the ball was an off-break, you instinctively pushed your hands, and therefore bat, a little bit away from you because the ball seemed so far to the off of you. This left

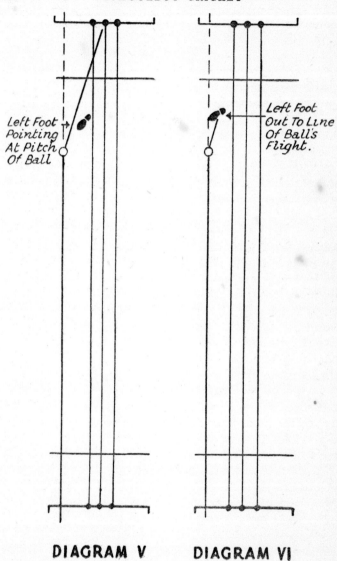

Left Foot Pointing At Pitch Of Ball

Left Foot Out To Line Of Ball's Flight.

DIAGRAM V   **DIAGRAM VI**

the fatal gap, and you were bowled. On the other hand, if the ball did not break you were playing it with the bat still farther away from you. Your eyes were far off the line, and you had not full control of the bat. You played it with the edge and were caught in the slips.

The remedy seems to be to play it as in Diagram VI. Instead of aiming your foot at the spot upon which you think the ball will pitch, you take it across to the off, just clear of an imaginary line which is an extension of the line of flight. You cannot reach that line when pointing your foot at the pitch of the ball, because it is too far away at that angle; but you can comfortably reach that line if you throw your foot more towards Point, as it were. The Diagram VI will make this clearer than it is in words. Now you are in a good position. Your eyes are looking down the line of the flight of the ball and you can watch the ball right on to the bat. If the ball does not break, you are in a position to play it with the bat near the body and under full control. If it does break from the off, you play it in front of the leg *with the break*, more towards the on side. If you miss it you are not bowled, because it hits your pad; and you are not l.b.w., because your pad is on the off-side of the line of the wickets.

When you are batting you cannot think all this out; but what I have found a useful thought is to thrust the left leg farther to the off, and less down the wicket, than one would if aiming the leg at the pitch of the ball. You have to acquire judgment as to how much to do this. If the ball is nearly a half-volley, then very little. If it is short of a length, then a considerable amount. I have found this tip very valuable when actually playing in matches, and only wish I had realized it years earlier.

Now with regard to getting the left leg out and across you must be careful not merely to *put* the leg out. You must also swing your weight forward and across until your head is directly over your left foot. If you find it difficult to do this here are three tips, one of which should help you.

(1) Instead of thinking of your foot, think of swinging your left shoulder across. If you do this, the foot goes too, in order to keep your balance.

(2) Make your *head* lead on to the line of the ball. Shoulder and leg will fit into place.

(3) As you stand at the crease have your *right* toe pointing a little more towards "third man" instead of parallel with the crease. If tip No. 1 or 2 works, either is better than No. 3 for various other reasons.

The rolling ball practice described in Chapter 1, Part II, is very valuable as a method of learning to get the left foot across to the line of an off-ball.

(5) Watching the Ball

This is a short foundation to write about but is most important—in fact the others are useless without it. It is WATCH THE BALL. Watch it as if it were a dangerous snake approaching you. Watch it as if you were trying to read the maker's name on it. Watch it so hard that you can see whether or not it is spinning, and which way. And watch it with your head down. An old professional coach is said constantly to have cried out, "Smell the ball, sir, smell the ball!" Very good advice.

CHAPTER II

BATTING *(Continued)*

IF you were to build the Foundations given in the previous chapter and make them part of yourself, even with no further instruction, your batting would improve enormously. There are also, however, some hints on the making of the various strokes, and of the way to play certain balls and certain types of bowling, which I can give you.

As you get experienced, you must learn to watch the bowler's hand so that you can get a fair idea as to whether to expect an off-break, leg-break, googly, top-spinner, swinger, etc. You cannot expect to do that in the early days; but keep it in mind.

You have been told how to deal with off-breaks, in the section on getting your left or right leg across to the line of the ball, and of how you should play *with* the break. A good off-break bowler will often bowl round the wicket. This means that the balls will take a line from well to the leg side of the line between the wickets, will pitch between the wickets, and then, if they break, will "straighten out" and come towards the middle stump. If they do not break, they will go straight along the line of flight well to the off of the wicket. Diagram VII shows the two types of ball.

Do you see the danger? If you play forward (unless the ball is so well pitched up to you that you can hit it almost as soon as it pitches) as if it were going to follow Track 1, Diagram VII, when it is really on Track 2, you may easily hit it with only the edge of your bat and give a catch in the slips. If you play it as if it were on Track 2, but it was really on Track 1, you will have put your left leg across to the line of the ball and will be l.b.w. The answer to the

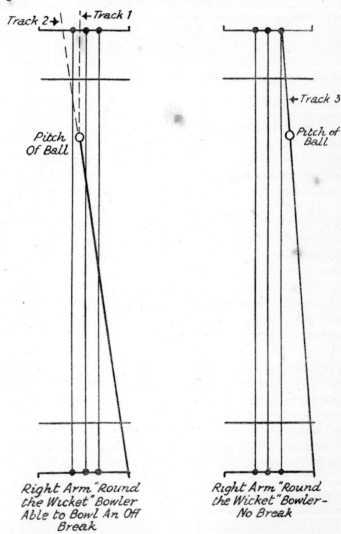

Track 2 ← Track 1

Pitch
Of Ball

← Track 3

Pitch of
Ball

Right Arm "Round
the Wicket" Bowler
Able to Bowl An Off
Break

DIAGRAM VII

Right Arm "Round
the Wicket" Bowler—
No Break

DIAGRAM VIII

problem is to play back, when possible, so that you will
have longer to watch the ball and to decide what it is
really doing.

Remember that it is safer to play back, to a fairly well-
pitched-up ball, when the bowler and pitch are slow,
than when they are fast.

There is another type of round-the-wicket bowler
that you will meet in Prep. School cricket. It is the boy
who bowls round the wicket because he finds he gets more
people out (a very sound reason), though he cannot bowl
off-breaks. He gets his wickets because the batsmen are
bad, and because a ball pitching outide the leg-stump
without break will probably hit the wicket. The simple
batsman thinks, "Hurrah! here's a leg ball," sweeps his
bat round to leg and is most surprised to find himself
bowled. The ball was an ordinary straight ball from where
it was bowled and took Track 3 on the Diagram VIII.

Now here is a tip against such folk. Get the Umpire
to give you guard from the place where the bowler's hand
is when he delivers the ball. Then forget about the actual
position of the bowler's end wicket but put it in imagina-
tion as if he were bowling over it. Turn your whole body
and stance to the left a corresponding amount, try to pick
out a mark or patch on the grass, which would be on the
line drawn from the imaginary wicket's off-stump to your
own leg-stump, and treat any ball which is not to the left
of that spot as a straight ball. In other words you play
him as an ordinary non-breaking over-the-wicket bowler
on the new line.

This brings me to the question of playing leg-balls
(of which there are many in Prep. School cricket) and of
genuine leg-breaks, which are comparatively rare.

It is heartrending to the batsman and his Cricket
Master to see leg-ball after leg-ball missed, which is
another way of saying boundary after boundary missed.

This is generally because boys try to make the bat chase the ball past their legs—and the bat seldom catches up. They also fail to get into a good hitting position.

Now I am going to tell you how to play a stroke which will give you bags of runs in Prep. School cricket, but it must be used only for short balls pitching outside the leg-stump.

The l.b.w. rule for balls pitching outside the leg-stump is quite different from the rule for those pitching outside the off-stump. IF A BALL PITCHES OFF THE WICKET ON THE LEG SIDE YOU CANNOT BE OUT L.B.W.

Therefore you can safely put your legs in front of the wicket. As I say, the ball pitches short and on the leg side. It is either going straight on and is a long hop to leg, or it is a leg-break and might hit the wicket. Never mind which it is for the first movement, which is to take the right foot back and across until it is a little way in front of your off-stump, meanwhile turning so that the toe points down the wicket towards the bowler. While you are doing this you are watching the ball, and by the time you have done it you have decided whether or not it is breaking on to the wicket.

If it is *not* breaking you bring back your left foot level with the right foot but keep it well to the leg side. You are now firmly planted on your feet, *legs apart*, facing the bowler's end; in a grand position for seeing the ball, and for giving it such a clout with a cross or horizontal bat, as it has seldom had: past square-leg, or over his head —and over the boundary too, if you feel confident enough.

If, however, by the time you have moved your right foot into position you have decided that the ball is a leg-break, you bring back your left leg level with the right as before, but this time close to your right leg. The two legs

PLATE 3. A bad stance. Weight is on the left leg, shoulders turned round so that chest faces the bowler, right foot too far behind crease, right knee in the way when bat is raised. Compare with Plate 4.

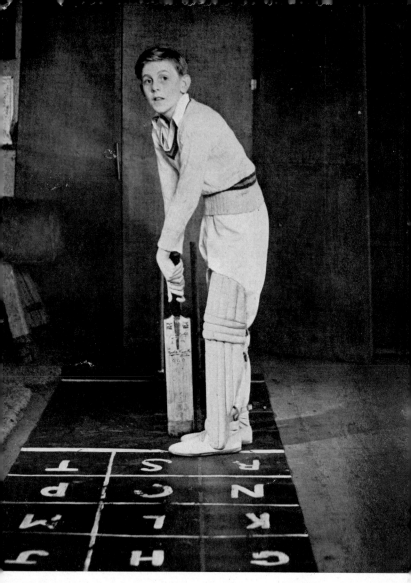

PLATE 4. A sensible stance. Note eyes nearly level, fully facing bowler, good position of hands, weight about equally divided between feet, right foot close to crease, *left foot slightly nearer the off side* (important). The stance could be bettered by chest not being so visible to bowler—provided the head position is not changed.

completely cover the wicket, and you can be neither bowled nor l.b.w., however good the ball. You do not try to clout this one—being a genuine leg-break it has probably gathered speed off the pitch—but push it off your legs with an upright bat. If you miss it—no matter; you are not l.b.w. (Study Plates VI and VII.)

The face of the bat should be a little to the left of mid-on. The speed of the ball and the angle of the bat will cause the ball to go more to the on than that. With experience you can vary this angle according to the position of the fieldsmen. Anyway, it is a golden rule to play leg-balls more towards the bowler's end than you intend them to go. You are also more likely to hit them as you are playing more down the line of flight.

Now with regard to *well pitched-up balls* clear of the leg-stump: just put your left leg to the ball and play it as you do straight- or off-balls. Make sure your head leads and your left shoulder drops.

But if the ball is a genuine leg-break, move smoothly down the wicket and play it before it pitches; it can't break if it does not pitch. Do not try to clout it, but push it carefully for one run, clear of the fieldsmen. One run per ball is 120 per hour, and that is very fast scoring. No leg-bowler likes this treatment, and he soon drops one short. There's your chance for four instead of one. Here is a golden rule for playing leg-breaks—"Right out or right back". Never scrape forward.

The ball rather wide on the off must be treated with care. The rule that you should put the left leg to the line of the ball is true only to balls which are not *very* wide; because if you put the leg to a very wide one and play the *ordinary straight bat shot*, your bat will be swinging in the direction of point—that is across the flight of the ball. You probably will not hit it; and if you do, it will very likely be a catch.

C

NO—if it is very wide and a half-volley or well pitched-up ball, leave it alone.

If it is a short ball, and it rises high—leave it alone.

If it is a very short ball and does not rise high it ought to be a boundary. Put your left leg straight across, but not too far, and slash downwards and across with the arms fairly straight, the face of the bat somewhat towards the ground, the right wrist rolling over the left as the ball is hit and the general course of the bat from high to low. You hit the ball on the top. This keeps it down and gives it top-spin which makes it streak for the boundary, probably past cover-point's left hand. If the ball is not quite so short, do the same shot, but with the right leg across instead of the left across. (See Plate VIII.)

A very common and dangerous fault with boys is the moving backwards towards square-leg to balls coming straight for the legs. If you do that and hit the ball, you have turned it into a "straight" ball (to you) and it is easily fielded by the bowler or mid-on. If you miss it, the ball may hit one of the pads and be deflected on to the wicket (Out!). Never draw away to leg.

Running

Some boys do not seem to realize that they go out to the wicket to make runs. Dozens of runs are missed from *slowly* hit balls; but when a boy hits a good hard smack, *off* he goes—and often *out* he goes. This is a natural feeling. You have felt a good hard hit on your bat, and it seems certain there must be a run; but you must get other ideas to seem natural in your head. If you hit the ball slowly it will take a long time to reach the fielder; and if your partner is backing up, and you always move forward after making your stroke, there is probably time for a run. It

often pays handsomely to run some short runs, because
the fielder may throw in hurriedly and wildly, crediting
you with an overthrow boundary. At any rate, it will tend
to make the fielders close in to stop the short ones, and
that makes it easier to hit the ball past them.

Back up if you are non-striker, be on the forward
move if you are the striker; in either case, run hard and
slide your bat in. Do not forget that if your bat is over
the crease but in the air, you are out. *On* the line is
out.

When you turn for another run slide your bat only
just in, turn and move out a yard or so before you or your
partner decide whether there is another run or not. Many
boys stand in an eager attitude, but with the bottom of the
bat still behind the line, though the ball is still forty yards
away, and cry, "Coming again?" Why not be two or
three yards down the pitch when you ask? The answer is
so much more likely to be a safe "Yes".

Calling is a bit of a problem. The general rule is that
the one whose danger it is should call, but whose is the
greater danger is not always easy to decide. If the ball
goes towards fine-leg, square-leg or past slips and wicket-
keeper it is obviously the non-striker's call. If it goes to
extra cover, past mid-off, bowler or mid-on it is equally
obviously the striker's call. It is the betwixt and betweens
that are the problem (i.e. to cover-point and mid-wicket).
Batsmen who are frequently in together seem to develop
a sort of telepathy, but in the ordinary way, every ball
should be called. In *doubtful* cases I think it should be left
to the striker to call, because the other player is probably
a yard or two down the wicket already and is on the move.
But do call clearly and loudly, and stick to your decision;
and if the other man has called, obey the call and run
like a hare.

Every rule is subject to exceptions; and it is quite in

order for an experienced player, whose stay at the wicket is vital at that stage of the match, to send back and even to sacrifice the inexperienced caller.

THE CLOCK

Boys do not, in the general way, appreciate the importance of the time as it relates to the state of the game. What is good play in certain conditions is poor play in others. An example will make this clear. In one of our School matches, when we were opposed by good bowling and keen fielding, one of our opening batsmen was in for two hours for 10 runs. He took an hour over his first two runs, but his innings up to that point was of great value, because at the other end the score was being pushed along at a reasonable rate. His eight in the second hour was a calamity. The good batsmen had gone and another sticker had come in. We had not enough runs on the board to declare, yet we were leaving ourselves perilously little time to get the opponents out. At last he got out. The next batsmen rattled up a few quick ones, but it was too late. When the last over of the day came, their shaky No. 11 was in; but we could not dislodge him, and the result was a draw.

Had that boy, after his first valuable hour, begun gradually to force the pace he would have made some runs or got out; and either solution would have been a blessing. I am not for a moment suggesting that he was selfish. He just did not realize the situation.

Sometimes a practice called "farming the bowling" should be used. This means that the faster scorer or safer batsman (whichever is the more important in the situation) should try to get as much of the bowling as possible, and the other fellow as little as possible. It is important that they should both carefully count the balls of each over.

Let us suppose that it is desirable that A should have as much and B as little of the bowling as possible. The first thing is that B must know of the plan. He can hardly be expected to co-operate if he is not told, and being less experienced than A he will probably not realize it himself. A faces the bowling. For the first four balls he tries to hit noughts, twos, fours or sixes; but no ones or threes. Off the fifth ball he tries to score a single. If he fails he can have another try off the sixth ball and so face the bowling at the other end. If he succeeds off the fifth ball, B has to face the last ball of the over only, and he must not score a single or run a bye. If A failed to score a single off the fifth or sixth ball B finds himself facing the first ball of the new over. He should, even at some risk, try to score a single so that A can have the bowling.

A PUZZLING CASE

Sometimes, to a straight ball which does not break, a batsman may lift his bat correctly, bring it down on the line of the ball, get his left foot correctly into position with his head down and on the line, no gap between bat and pad, perfectly straight bat—and yet get bowled. Most puzzling and disappointing! Everything was done right (so he thinks) and yet he is out. Yes! everything else was done right, but one wrong thing had crept in which made all the right things useless. Instead of telling you what it was now, I want you first to get a bat and try the following experiment. It will show you the fault better than a long description.

Take up your correct position as if batting, raise your bat and play *very slowly* a forward defensive shot as if to a straight ball; but stop when the bat is just an inch or so short of level with your left leg. Now look down at your bat, and still watching your bat, let your right hip come forward by allowing your right foot to turn on to the toe with the instep now pointing towards the bowler, and continue the stroke by pushing the bat just beyond your leg.

If you watch your bat carefully you will see that the whole bat, whilst remaining perfectly upright, moves two or three inches to the left. That is why the batsman was bowled. The position of the right foot and hip which I have described is often seen in photographs of famous players as the *finish* of a forward stroke or drive. **Quite right; it is the finish. And the whole point is that the right foot should not be allowed to turn from its position of being *parallel with the crease* (though the heel may rise for comfort) until the bat has actually hit the ball.**

The instant you feel that you have "connected", you can allow the right foot to turn and the right hip to come forward for the follow-through. Now do the experiment with right foot action correct, and watch how the blade of your bat remains true on its course until it is just past your leg, by which time you would actually have hit the ball. (Plates IX and X show this experiment.)

I consider this one of the most important tips in the book, because the cause of getting out is so subtle; and yet what a world of difference between having hit the ball and being bowled—not once but on numerous occasions.

You will remember that I said in Chapter 1 that I would tell you when and how to develop the muscular memory. The answer is—in the winter, and by slow-motion practice. Plates IX and X illustrate this slow-motion practice with the numbered mat.

I play the piano, and if I want to learn a very fast piece of music, I practice it slowly, *very slowly*, telling my

hands and fingers carefully what they have to do and
feeling the movements. The same applies to batting. Tell your
muscles what they have to do, let them do it slowly, feel
them doing it. Then—in actual play—they will do
the same things, without thought and at lightning
speed.

CHAPTER III

BOWLING

IF, on a country walk, you come across a pond with a tin can floating in the middle, what do you do? Unless you are very different from me, you look around for a stone to bung at it. Ah! there's a suitable one, about the size of a golf ball. You throw it, and probably hit the tin— or nearly do so. You look round again and cannot see another of that size. You pick up a pebble as big as a marble and have a shot with that. Again you nearly hit the can. There are no more stones, but you see an old brick which you pick up. This is too heavy to chuck overhand so you swing it underhand. Bang it goes on the top of the tin with a lovely, satisfying sound, and down they both go to the bottom.

Now this is all very wonderful, because your muscles are doing something they have never done before. They have never thrown a stone of exactly the weight of the first stone exactly that distance. Then they must adjust themselves to the much smaller weight of the pebble; and an entirely different set of muscles is at work when you throw the heavy brick underhand.

The accuracy of your three throws is only *probable* if you have done much throwing in your time, and only *possible* if you look hard at the tin can and really aim at it.

This little story is a good illustration of two Foundations of Bowling, viz: *practice* and *aiming* at a particular spot on the pitch. The bowler has the advantage of having a ball of the same weight and size each time. This is a third Foundation and I am going to write of them in reverse order, before dealing with the vitally important fourth foundation.

(1) The Ball

No boy under the age of fourteen should ever bowl with a full-sized ball (5½ ozs.). It is too big and too heavy. The boys' size ball weighs 4¾ ozs. and, if it has been made by an acknowledged manufacturer, will be of the correct size.

(2) Aiming

I have asked many beginners whether they aim at a definite spot on the pitch or "just bowl". The answer is generally a rather embarrassed "Just bowl, sir". Merely being asked that question is enough to tell them how silly it is to expect to be accurate if they are not even aiming! But boys who are past the beginner's stage often do not aim with sufficient concentration, and they frequently do not know where to aim in the particular circumstances.

(3) Practice

There is nothing much to be said about this except that there must be plenty of it. Of course x hours of practice on a good plan is worth more than $3x$ hours without a plan.

(4) Length

This is really the Foundation of all; but my Foundations 1, 2 and 3 had to be built in order to build and form parts of this all-important Foundation. "Length" means the distance from the batsman to the spot where the ball pitches; and the bowler who can say he has mastered length is one who is accurate in pitching the ball where he wants to, *and* who knows how far from the batsman he should pitch it in the particular circumstances of the moment. Pace and swerve and break and top-spin and flight are all valuable weapons for a bowler to possess in his battle with the batsman, but they are useless without length; just as a revolver, a coal-hammer and a rope are valuable weapons against a burglar, but are useless if you go to the wrong room. You would stand a better chance of catching him if you went, with bare hands, to the right room. *Length* is, as it were, the right room. Few boys realize the tremendous value of length. On the hard Australian wickets, upon which it is difficult to make the ball break, slow bowlers such as Wilfred Rhodes and J. C. White were able to keep the world's best batsmen quiet by bowling just length.

Therefore a boy who can bowl a length, even though his "action" is full of faults is a good and valuable bowler. If the faults can be removed and he can still bowl a length he is a more valuable bowler. Length is difficult to explain because of the infinite variety of circumstances; but I will do my best. Remember, I am not talking now about direction, which is also important. I will give you some examples which may help you to an idea of what length is; after which you should be able to work out other examples for yourself.

Whether or not a ball pitching on a certain spot is of good length depends upon the speed of the bowler, the state of the wicket (hard, soft, fiery, sticky, etc.), the state of the game (whether it is more important to keep down runs or to get wickets), the height and reach of the batsman, the style and temperament of the batsman, and so on and so on.

Before we think of the examples let us consider what balls are not (generally) good length. A full-pitcher, a half-volley and a long hop are all easy balls to hit for runs, so they are not of good length. The pitch of a good length ball must therefore lie between that of the half-volley and that of the long hop; but that is a fairly big distance, and the problem is how far along that strip to pitch them.

Imagine you are bowling to two batsmen, A and B. You soon realize that A is good and safe in his forward shots, but B is much better when playing back. A good length to one is not a good length to the other. *The best length to any batsman is a ball to which he does not know whether to play forward or back.* Your good length ball to A will therefore be shorter than your good length ball to B. The same sort of situation will probably occur when one batsman is much taller, and can reach farther down the pitch than the other. In this example you have the same conditions of pitch, but different types of batsman.

Now consider the case of the batsman to whom you often bowl. You have here the same batsman, but different conditions from day to day. On a hard, fast, true wicket he can safely play forward to balls which are fairly short, and your good length ball will be just shorter than that. But if you pitched your ball on the same spot when the wicket was slow and soft, it would be an easy long hop and would probably be hit to the boundary. On a sticky wicket even well pitched-up balls will often pop up sharply (bounce high) and if you have tempted the batsman to play forward by bowling well up to him he may offer an easy catch.

In the ordinary way, a half-volley is a bad length ball against good batsmen; but it is often a good length ball against bad ones. In Prep. School cricket, when you have dismissed five or six pretty good players, there often appears a large boy with a deep bass voice and budding moustache, looking about seventeen years old. His Cricket Master hurries over to your Master to tell him that the boy is really only just thirteen. This boy is generally a poor batsman, being slow in his movements; but he hits the ball very hard, generally high over wide mid-on's head.

He is particularly severe on your good length balls with a slight off-break. His bat swings across the line of the ball, hitting it on the rise and with the break. Of course, you have a fielder at long-on, but there is much space in those parts and the long, high hits may continue to fall just out of reach. In a few minutes he is turning his side's very moderate position into a good one.

He must go. He probably will if you bowl him a straight *half-volley* just a shade slower (or faster) than the balls you have been giving him. The ball is pitched too far up for him to watch it off the pitch, he plays a little too soon (or late) owing to the ball being of *slightly* different pace (don't make it obvious) and as he is playing across the flight he misses the ball and is bowled. So in this case a half-volley is a good length ball!

There is another time when a half-volley may be a good length ball even to a good batsman if he is hitting rather freely. A half-volley, *rather wide on the off*—and, if possible, going away farther after pitching, will often cause him to mishit and so give a catch to extra-cover or cover.

Sometimes good length bowling plays a batsman in rather than out. He solemnly pats back ball after ball, making no attempt to score, but all the time he is getting himself used to the light and the pace of the pitch. In an hour's time he may be hitting the bowling all over and out of the ground. "Such men are dangerous". So do not give him too much of it without trying a long hop or a half-volley on the off. He is only human, and he would like to see a few runs on the board and may therefore have a fatal crack at one of the "bad" balls!

The last few examples seem to be more under the heading of bowling tactics than length, but I find it hard to know where the dividing line between these subjects should come.

Well, there are your real foundations—aiming, practice, length. There is also, however, the importance of developing a good action. I will deal with this, but first let me clear out of the way two matters—the length of the pitch and the grip of the ball. Just as no Prep. schoolboy should use a full-sized ball, so he should never bowl on a full-sized pitch. The recognized length for Prep. Schools is 21 yards. In games below the first game it should be less.

The Grip

Never hold the ball in the palm of the hand. It is generally only the keenest boys who do this, and the reason is that, because they are so keen, they try to bowl when they are very young and tiny, and can hold the ball in no other way. Now there are grips for off-breaks, leg-breaks, in-swingers, out-swingers and so on, and just to show that there is always a chance of something new being discovered, take the case of the Australian, Jack Iveson, aged thirty-four, who bowled very well for Melbourne last season and who is being talked about as a possibility for Inter-State and even International Cricket. Now Iveson is said to hold the ball only between his thumb and first finger, and to be able to impart plenty of spin with accuracy.

I am not going to attempt to describe or illustrate all

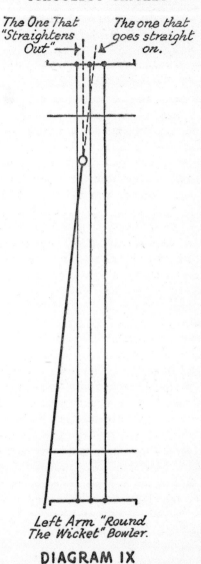

The One That "Straightens Out" →

The one that goes straight on.

Left Arm "Round The Wicket" Bowler.

DIAGRAM IX

these grips. This book is to help you to build foundations. When you have built these, you can study the many fine books of instruction by famous cricketers, in which you will find photographs, description and advice. But I do urge you first to get the foundations and to use a general purpose finger grip such as is illustrated in Plate XIV.

It is true that it is better to bowl well with a bad action than badly with a good one, but better still to bowl well with a good action. By "good" I mean an action which gives the best results with the least effort. This is most important, because it is not of any great use to be able to bowl well for only a very few overs. Some bowlers tear up to the wicket, hurl themselves in the air and sling the ball down with all their might. The ball travels moderately fast through the air, hits the pitch like a lump of suet pudding and then comes in at a harmless, easy pace. This is often called "friendly bowling" by cricketers. Others run up in an easy manner and swing the ball down in an almost leisurely way, yet it travels through the air almost as fast as the other type, and when it hits the pitch it fairly fizzes off. In what does the difference lie?

It is, I think, largely a matter of timing. A cricket-ball is not bowled by the arms alone, and a good bowler uses the impetus of his run up, his legs, body, arms, wrist and even fingers to propel the ball. He also times or fits all these movements smoothly together. The poor bowler either leaves out some of these factors or mistimes them.

Now my first strong recommendation to you is not to try to bowl too fast, even if you are the School's fast bowler. If you overdo it, you will not only fail to time your movements but you will not last. Think of a motor-car designed to do a maximum speed of 65 m.p.h. You could cruise at 50–55 m.p.h. for days on end without hurting it, and you could still push up to the 65 occasionally for a little while. But if you kept it constantly at 65 m.p.h. it would soon be ruined. So with your bowling. If you are a fast bowler, bowl at your fast cruising-speed and keep your fastest ball for occasional use. You will not only last longer, but the surprise of the extra fast one will sometimes get a wicket.

My second recommendation is that you should find, by experiment, the shortest run that suits you; measure it carefully and stick to it. More detailed advice on this subject and on the important details of a good action are to be found in the chapter on Bowling in Part II. If you are reading this book in the Winter I advise you to work at those details with your master or with a friend. You can stand opposite each other but sideways-on as if bowling at each other, and check the positions one by one. Later you can bowl a soft rubber ball (if indoors) at each other, again checking each other's positions.

But if, as is quite likely, you are reading this book in the Spring, you must be careful (if you are already a bowler) not to alter too much at a time or you may, temporarily, spoil your bowling. If done very carefully, however, you can greatly improve your bowling even during the season. To do this just alter one thing at a time slightly. In Part II, p. 103, you will see that I suggest that the master should get into the wicket-keeper's position and look for ten points in the bowler's action.

Now, unless you are already doing it, why not be sure that you just practise raising that left arm high and straight just before you deliver the ball? (Point 2) When that has become natural to you, see about No. 3. Look at the batsman behind that high straight arm. When this has become automatic you will find No. 1 is already correct, for you can hardly look behind a high straight arm unless you are sideways on to the batsman. It is quite likely that No. 5 will also be automatically correct and that, in its turn, will make No. 6 satisfactory. Thus

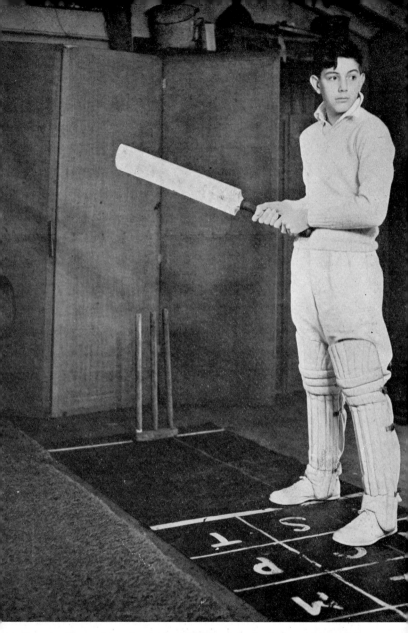

PLATE 5. How *not* to raise the bat! Weight on heels, body straightened, bat
pointing at "third man". The batsman can do nothing but hit across the
flight of the ball.

PLATE 6. Hitting a long-hop pitching off the wicket on the leg side, and *not* breaking. This position is good, but could be better—because more powerful—if the legs are slightly more bent at the knees.

by attending to two points you will have got six correct.

There is also a list of five points on page 104 which the master is asked to look for from the position of mid-on. No. 5 is very easy to introduce during the actual season, and may very greatly increase your ease of bowling and effectiveness. I consider it so important that a full explanation is worth while and will help you. Before giving you the explanation, I want you to know that some years ago I had a boy who generally had to bowl uphill on our ground. Though he pitched the balls well up, they seemed to have a job to reach the wicket. After explaining this bit of wrist work to him and giving him a couple of turns in the nets at it he tried it with much success in a match. He took several wickets and his balls, up the hill, were really slapping into the wicket-keeper's hands when the batsman missed them.

Now for the explanation. Imagine you are standing in the corridor of a railway coach, facing the engine. The train is going at 60 m.p.h., so *you personally* are passing the telegraph posts at 60 m.p.h. Suppose you wish to pass these posts personally at 64 m.p.h. for a moment or two. Which is the easier way to get your wish—to arrange for the engine-driver and firemen to coax another 4 m.p.h. out of the engine (it may be beyond its powers) or for you simply to walk forward at 4 m.p.h. down the corridor? You personally are now passing the telegraph posts at 64 m.p.h. Obviously that is the easier way.

Now back to bowling. Your arm is the train, your fingers holding the ball are you. Just make your fingers go faster than your arm and you have added the speed of that movement to the speed of your arm. To do this you simply bend your wrist forward as you bowl. To bend it forward you must first have bent it back. That is what is meant by the wrist being "flexed backwards at the bottom of the right arm's swing". (Point 5, p. 104).

D

I would add one further remark to this. Movement is better if it comes from a previous movement. That is why we do not start a cricket bat's, a golf club's, a tennis racket's swing from a stationary raised position. So with the backward bending of the wrist. Bend it forward as you take your right hand down to its lowest position, bend it back there and forward again as you bowl.

You can easily see what a powerful "extra" the wrist can be if you will try this test. Stand as if bowling to a wicket with a ball in your fingers and the right arm still and stretched fully upwards. Then, without moving your arm at all, bend back your wrist and bowl the ball with a forward movement of the wrist only. You will be surprised how far the ball will go, and if you allow a very small movement of the arm, you will discover you can bowl it the full length of the pitch. I am asking you to add this movement to the movement of your arm in ordinary bowling. For a very short time your length will suffer, but after a little while you will have recovered length and be bowling a far more lively ball.

A word to left-handers. As soon as you can bowl a length, learn the off-break grip. That will be a leg-break to the batsman. Then, bowling round the wicket, you will be able to vary your balls between those going straight on (and therefore coming in from the off to the batsman) and those which break back and "straighten out" or even go a little towards the slips. (See Diagram IX on p. 46.) You can imagine that the batsman has to exercise a great deal of care in dealing with good length bowling of this type. I will conclude this chapter on bowling with a short story. "Not much of a story" you may say. Well, it has a point! I wonder whether you will see it?

A boy was one of the opening bowlers in a Prep. School XI for three years in succession, and against their strongest opponents he took the first two wickets each year. When he had taken his second wicket the first year he said, "Good, I've taken two wickets already". The second year he said, "That's good—two wickets down— I'm glad *I* took them". On the third occasion he simply said, "Hurrah! that's two of them out of the way".

CHAPTER IV

FIELDING

WHAT'S that? Did I hear you say "Fielding is awfully boring, sir!" Good heavens, boy, haven't you ever fielded?

Fielding is watching a game of cricket at close quarters. Fielding is being part of that game. Fielding is watching your own bowlers and trying to guess their plans, and helping them to carry out those plans. Fielding is watching the batsman, possibly learning from him, looking for his weaknesses, estimating from what kind of ball and stroke you will get a catch or one to field. Fielding is anticipating the ball that is coming to you, so that you are there first and make a good catch, or stop a hot shot and hurl it to the wicket-keeper to run out the batsman. Fielding is supporting your bowlers and the captain so keenly that they give of their best.

No, I did not really think you said that. I think you said, "Slack fielding is awfully boring, sir!" Quite right; it is. Now for the foundations:

(1) Avoiding Tension

Tension means tight muscles, and unless you are careful to avoid it, your very keenness may make you tighten up your arms and hands, even your whole body. This is particularly likely when you are fielding close in at such places as slip, gully, point, silly mid-off, silly mid-on, or short-leg. In these positions you do not move in as the ball is bowled, as you should in other positions. You lean forward with your hands in front of you, weight on toes. At times it is easy to get tense without realizing it. Personally, just as the bowler was delivering the ball, I used always to give my hands, wrists, arms and even body a tiny loose shake; not enough to be seen by other people, but just enough to assure myself that there was no stiffness. If your muscles are stiff when a catch comes to you, you will almost certainly drop it.

(2) Speed

We all vary as to the speed with which we can make movements, and all that I can say is that you should take a pride in being as quick as you possibly can. If you are chasing a ball to the boundary and feel sure you cannot catch it you should, nevertheless, run at your top speed. It helps to keep the atmosphere and the other fielders keen and alert. Keenness and slackness are both infectious.

If a ball is coming towards you when you are fielding some way from the wicket you should simply tear in towards the ball. It looks well, and may frighten the batsmen from taking a perfectly safe run. One run saved is as good as making a run when batting, and if through your speed you catch out their No. 3 batsman, it is often as useful as if you had made 50 or 100 runs.

All fielders except those close in should be on the forward move as the ball is bowled. This enables them to get away after the ball much more quickly than if they stand still. It is a mistake, however, to be *running* in as the ball leaves the bowler's hands, as it takes too long to change direction.

(3) Anticipation

If, however, by observing the kind of ball that is going down the pitch, and the batsman's footwork and movements, you get a pretty good idea as to where the ball is likely to go, you can start off running in that direction as hard as you like. This often makes all the difference between one run and four. I have known a good slip fielder to a slow bowler sometimes move forward quite calmly and practically take the ball off the poor batsman's bat. He has seen from the bowler's hand and from the flight of the ball that it will pitch in a certain spot and turn away. He has also taken a mental photograph of the batsman's footwork, and the way he is shaping for his stroke. He knows that the ball will come gently off the edge of the bat, and moves forward to catch it just before it drops to the ground two feet away from the bat. I am not suggesting he thinks all this out consciously. He is a born cricketer with a vast experience; and the wonderful instrument which is his mind uses all the factors in a lightning calculation, so that he seems to move forward and put his hand out instinctively. But he would not have reached this happy state had he not always been keen and tried to develop his powers of anticipation.

(4) "Give"

If you throw a ball at a hard wall it will bounce back towards you. If you throw it against a hanging curtain the part of the curtain which the ball hits will move back slightly and the ball will drop straight down in a lifeless manner. That is what I mean by "give", and it is not a big movement. There is a good and interesting way of practising this "give" which is most important in catching and fielding. If your muscles are tight the ball will bounce out; and if it has not bounced out but you grip it too tightly, it is quite possible that it may be squeezed out.

Try throwing up the ball, at first only a little way, and catching it with your fingers apart. Do not grip the ball at all or even close your fingers. You will soon find you can catch quite high and hard catches this way. Practise with each hand separately and with both together. To show that the gripping is not necessary, and that it is only a question of the right "give", I have learned to catch quite high balls on the face of a bat, and that can't grip, can it? It is an amusing and instructive trick which you may care to practise at home and then astonish the other boys at school.

Of course, in a match or game you would close your fingers over the ball as an extra precaution, and you should always do so to some balls when you are practising catching by "give" only. This will teach you the timing of the closing of the fingers; you will be surprised how small the "give" movement is.

Now for some general hints on fielding. (I am assuming you are a right-handed thrower.) The difference in time between a batsman's being "in" or "out" by an inch is a very minute fraction of a second, and you must try to save those fractions of seconds where possible, by picking up the ball in such a way that you are ready to throw, and by throwing in such a way that the ball comes easily to the wicket-keeper's hands (or bowler's) either full pitch just over the stumps or *long hop* if you are too far away to reach him full pitch.

Avoid, above all things, throwing so that the ball comes to him half-volley—that is at the bottom of the stumps. How far away from him you should pitch the ball depends upon how hard you can throw and the condition of the ground. You must thus take into consideration how soft or hard the field is and how closely the grass has been cut.

First, let us imagine that you are fielding at cover, or deep mid-off, or deep mid-on. The batsman plays the ball very slowly towards you and calls for a run. You must dash in, and without checking your speed, bend down and flick the ball underhand to the wicket-keeper (full pitch, of course) as smartly as you can. Try to avoid even bending back the wrist for the flick but make the whole thing one movement. Do not worry a bit if you misfield the ball or even miss it entirely. They cannot get more than one run anyway, and they have got that one run unless you run out one of them. Therefore the attempt at extreme speed is worth the risk.

With regard to really hard hits you must decide, from the state of the game, whether it is more important to take an outside chance of running out your man, with the possibility of a boundary if you misfield, or to make sure that only a single run can be taken owing to your safe fielding. If you are fielding at deep square-leg and the ball is hit towards the fine-leg boundary you must try to turn a four into a one by running hard and stopping the ball with your right hand and throwing in with an under-the-shoulder action. You can do this before you have even straightened the body from the pick-up, whereas if you use the ordinary over-the-shoulder throw you will have to straighten your body and turn a little towards the wicket. Remember, however, that in throwing, as in bowling, you should be sideways on to your objective and move your weight from your right leg to your left leg as you throw.

If you have to run from square-leg in the opposite direction you will stop the ball with your left hand, transfer it to your right as you pull up, turn round to the left so that you are ready to throw. In this case you will throw from the over-the-shoulder position.

This would, perhaps, be a good moment to give you another little tip. If you are responsible for a "front" of say 20 yards as a fielder, do not place yourself bang in the middle, because as a right-hander you can be quicker and more useful in the part of your "front" to the right. Therefore increase the ground to the right of you and decrease that which is to your left. In your 20 yards you might well divide it up into parts such as 8 yards to your left but 12 yards to your right. But, of course, go and stay where your captain puts you.

When you chase a ball, make sure you have really overtaken it before you stoop down to pick it up. If you are only just level with it when you stoop you will find that it has got ahead of you again. Having got a tiny bit ahead of the ball, you bend down as you run, getting your cupped hand in front of the ball just when your right foot is coming down on to the ground. The ball rolls into your hand and you straighten up and turn *to the left* ready to throw. By turning to the left you have only to turn a quarter-circle before you reach the throwing position; but if you turn to the right you have to move through three-quarters of a circle. I have seen young County players make this mistake.

So far I have only tried to teach you things of which I have had actual experience either as a player or a coach. Now I am about to pass on to you a tip which I heard only a week or two ago. I take no responsibility for it; but I think it must be sound, as the cricketer who told me is a sound player and coach. He said that when the ball comes fast to your left, so that you have to stop it with out-stretched left hand, pass the ball *behind your back* to your right hand which is then automatically in a position to make an immediate throw without any wind-up.

To stop very hard shots straight at you, in such positions as mid-off, put your heels together, toes at an angle, bend down, cup your hands between your feet, and watch the ball right into your hands. If the hit is very hard to your right side, thrust out your right foot at right angles to the line of the ball's approach (as if you were going to stop it with your foot), put your cupped right hand by your instep to receive the ball, at the same time going down on to the grass, or nearly so, with your left knee and have your left hand ready to close on the ball. *Vice versa* to balls on your left. Never, till you are over 50, stop a ball with your foot. You have a waist which will bend, haven't you? Cricketers over fifty years of age sometimes have not; but you should have seen J. B. Hobbs at that age fielding cover-point!

When you are about to throw, always keep an eye on each wicket. How many times in our School matches has one of the boys dashed in, picked up the ball smartly and thrown in like a bullet, but to the wrong end, where the batsman has just arrived! Meanwhile the other batsman is only two-thirds of the way down the pitch. If chances of a run out seem equal, choose the wicket-keeper's end, as he has gloves and pads; but if there seems more chance at the bowler's end throw to him. He should be waiting, with the wicket between you and himself, ready to take the ball and put down the wicket (i.e. knock off the bails).

Remember that you do not have to throw the ball if you are at the wicket. Knock off the bails with your hand or hands provided you are at the time holding the ball. If the bails are already off, for any reason, you can run the man out by pulling up a stump with the ball in your hand or hands.

When another fielder is throwing in, be sure to "back up". This means that you must get behind the wicket-keeper or bowler who is waiting to receive the ball, in case he misses it. Do not get too close to him or you may miss it too. If there is another fielder anywhere near he should be behind you.

With regard to catching, you should never use one hand if you can conveniently use two to the ball and you should try to get your eyes as much in line with the ball's approach as possible. Very hard-hit catches straight at your middle, such as often come to mid-on, are difficult, as you cannot let your hands give. You should move your body to the side, keeping your eyes on the line of the ball, and take it at the side of, but close to, your body. When it is a low, skimming catch you should get your head low— don't just put down your hands. For high, dropping catches cup your hands as near eye level as possible. If you cup the hands at waist level your eyes cannot follow the last yard of the ball's flight. Never have your fingers pointing up like a crocodile's mouth. You will either get your fingers broken or bruise the heel of your hand and, in any case, you will miss the catch. This applies equally to low catches coming at you.

When you are fielding at 2nd slip, gully or point do not watch the ball down the pitch. Watch the bat all the time. If the eyes have been following the ball down the wicket and the batsman edges it, they cannot adjust themselves quickly enough to the new angle taken by the ball. 1st slip, being so much more on the line, should, however, watch the ball from the bowler's hand and be ready even to run behind the wicket-keeper to the fine leg position.

Finally, do not wander about according to where the last ball has been hit. The bowler may have a plan! The captain may not be a half-wit! You can move from your post, in anticipation, as the ball is bowled and the batsman shapes; but do not alter the position of fielding at *your* discretion. That is the captain's job; though the bowler may ask him to shift a man.

I cannot resist ending this chapter on fielding with accounts of two wonderful examples which I saw some years ago. In 1938 I watched every ball of the Test Match at the Oval when England made 903 for 7 wickets declared (Hutton 364). For the whole of that immense innings which took, so far as I can remember, nearly three days, Hassett was fielding at deep extra-cover and throwing in from the boundary full pitch to the wicket-keeper. My memory is that the keeper never had to move his feet to take Hassett's throws, which all came to him beautifully just over the top of the stumps. Hassett had his reward when, by a superb piece of fielding, he ran Leyland out.

A more recent and clearer memory is of a catch taken by W. R. Hammond in the slips during the "Victory Test" at Manchester in 1945. I was standing near the sight-screen at the striker's end, watching Pollard bowling at a pretty lively speed. One of the Australians just edged the ball, very fine, between the wicket-keeper and Hammond at 1st slip. A lesser fielder would have just had time to stick out his left hand in hope. The ball *might* have stuck. Not so Hammond. I had a perfect position for seeing him bring off the most glorious catch I have ever witnessed. He dived over to the left to get his eyes on the line of the ball, and as he fell, I saw his two hands cupped dead on the line waiting for the ball to be safely held. Never before or since have I been so perfectly placed to see a grand catch, being myself right on the line of the ball. Thus I had a mental photograph of Hammond's waiting hands.

CHAPTER V

WICKET–KEEPING

MYSELF a wicket-keeper of moderate standard I am, perhaps, particularly enthusiastic as to the joys of this position. In no other place can one see so much of the game. The keeper sees the bowler's action perfectly, observes the flight, swerve or spin of the ball and the batsman's movements. He has no dull periods. There is no ball bowled that he may not have to field or catch. He is concerned with the taking of the return throw from the fielder in the majority of cases and he has the occasional pleasure of relieving his feelings by bellowing "How's that?" There is no doubt but that some people are naturally meant to be wicket-keepers and others are not, and I strongly advise you to look for an opportunity to test yourself while you are still young. I had never kept wicket in my life until I was thirty-three, when an emergency caused me to put on pads and gloves. Naturally I did not "keep" well but my performance was sufficiently satisfactory for me to become the regular keeper, and in course of time, I reached the standard of keeping to first-class bowlers—and what a joy that is! It is quite certain that if I had started as a boy I should have been far better, and I wish I had been given a trial at school.

FOUNDATIONS
(1) Stance

The advice of most great keepers is that you should keep your heels on the ground when you bend or squat down, and from my own experience, I fully agree. It must be said, however, that there are certain first-class keepers playing today who crouch on their toes with heels off the ground. One of the dangers of this method is that you are *balancing* on your toes and you may put your finger-tips on the ground to help you to keep your balance— particularly if there is a strong wind. When you move your hands you may find yourself out of balance. In any case, if you are balanced, I do not think you can move in different directions so quickly as if you have a good, firm, flat-footed base. The lower you get your eyes the easier it is to see the ball; but you must be careful not to crouch or squat so low that you cannot move quickly. If you like a low position, it is best to avoid getting into it too soon, as the muscles do not then respond so quickly. In the case of keeping to a bowler who takes a longish run, you can stand up as he walks back, go halfway down as he starts his run, and get right down only just before he bowls. That it is not necessary for everyone to get low is told us by that great England wicket-keeper, Herbert Strudwick, who informs us that one of the best wicket-keepers he ever saw was M. W. Payne of Cambridge University, and that he stood straight up. He tells us also that the famous G. MacGregor, and Tilly and many others, just bent their backs. However, I still think the lower the better *provided*

(*a*) you do not cramp yourself;
(*b*) you rise soon enough to be in a comfortable and suitable position for taking the ball without a sense of flurry.

The feet should be well separated to give you a firm base and something to push from when you want quickly to go to left or right. You should be squarely facing the bowler; and a good position for the feet against normal bowling is to have the left toe behind the leg stump and the right foot to the off of the off-stump. When you squat down let your knees be wide apart, your arms and hands between them but *not* with your elbows resting on the upper part of your legs. This cramps their movements. The fingers should be pointing downwards. The hands should be close to each other but not quite touching, as this may cause tension. You have read what was said about the avoidance of tension (tight muscles) when fielding, and the same applies to wicket-keeping.

(2) "Give"

All that was said with regard to "give" in the chapter on fielding applies with even more force to wicket-keeping. The fielder may have to stop only a few hot shots in an innings, and the average of catches per fielder per innings would be less than one. Yet the wicket-keeper will probably have to take several balls per over; and unless he achieves the right "give", not only will he drop a number but also his hands will suffer. It is easy for him to get practice if he can find a keen bowler who also wants to practise. The keeper must try to avoid any kind of a snatch at the ball or any tension, but just let the ball come into his hands with the right amount of "give". Confidence and skill will soon come.

(3) Downward–pointing Fingers

A better description of this important principle would, in my opinion, be "away-from-the-centre-pointing-fingers"; but that would be a very clumsy title. What it really means is that the wicket-keeper should rise so that he can take any reasonably straight ball, which does not get up above his waist, with downward-pointing fingers.

If the ball rises chest-high, and he merely stands up and takes it in front of the chest, he can neither take it with downward-pointing fingers nor with the right "give". It will almost certainly bounce out.

The way to take this sort of ball is to move your body slightly to the left, and take the ball near the body with fingers pointing away from you to the right. You will see what I mean by "away-from-the-centre-pointing-fingers" if you consider the bottom of your breast-bone as the centre away from which your fingers should always point.

Very high balls will be taken with fingers pointing upwards and so on. It is very important that you should no more play across the flight of the ball with your hands than you do with your bat. If a ball is passing to your right you must not just thrust out your hands, however well you may be pointing your fingers, at the last moment. You must get them there early on the line of the ball so that it can come into them as they wait. The farther away you put your hands the farther from the line of the ball are your eyes. You should therefore move across to the line of the ball as far as you can, *without cramping your arms and hands* by having them too close to the body.

Those are the foundations; now for some detail. If a ball looks like passing the batsman on the off and keeping low, do not bring the pads together as a precaution in case you miss it with your hands. That forms a bad habit; and you will find yourself relying more and more on the pads, until you are no longer a wicket-keeper but merely a stopper. Move your right leg as far as you need in order to get your head on the line of the ball, keep your head forward and down, and take the ball with downward-pointing fingers. If necessary move your left leg also (backwards if the ball is over-pitched, as this makes it easier to keep your head down).

PLATE 7. A ball is pitched on the same spot as the leg long-hop but breaks in towards the wicket. The right leg goes to exactly the same place and position, but the left leg is brought back near to the right in order to guard the stumps. The batsman *cannot* be out l.b.w. to a ball pitching on the leg side. Note how well the batsman keeps his head down and how closely he watches the ball.

PLATE 8. The short, wide off ball which does not rise high is hit by this stroke. The ball cannot be shown, but would be nearly opposite the right leg. In a fraction of a second the right hand will roll over the left, the blade of the bat will turn its face more towards the ground, the wrists will cross with a snap. The picture, being posed, makes it appear a gentle shot, but it is really a terrific *slash*.

Above everything, do not feel yourself "stuck". In all games footwork is half the battle, and this applies to wicket-keeping. Get into the way of considering that the putting of the feet into position to make the other movements easy is the first thing to do. This does not mean that you should move *backwards* with both feet or you will be out of stumping range; but you can move one foot back to take an over-pitched ball which you think will pitch about level with the stumps.

In any case it is better if you can achieve the desired position by moving one foot only, for in wicket-keeping, as in batting, the last thing you want is to have your eyes bobbing up and down. Another advantage of keeping one foot in position is that you have a sort of anchor which tells you where the wicket is, in case you want to whip off the bails.

A most important detail is that to take a leg-ball you should not move to the left and *backwards* but should put your left leg to the left and slightly *forwards*. The nearer you are to the batsman the shorter the distance you have to move to see round him. Do not take the ball in front of the wicket, or your smart piece of stumping will be given "not out". (See Diagram XII on p. 66.)

UP OR BACK?

An important question, especially in Prep. School cricket, is whether the keeper should stand up to the wicket or back. For normal paced bowling the answer is undoubtedly up to the wicket. Boys (and cricketers in general) are very nervous of being stumped. If the batsman sees that the keeper is standing back, he not only knows that he cannot be stumped, but he has also a delightful feeling of confidence that he need not worry about dragging his back foot over the crease, or fear to

E

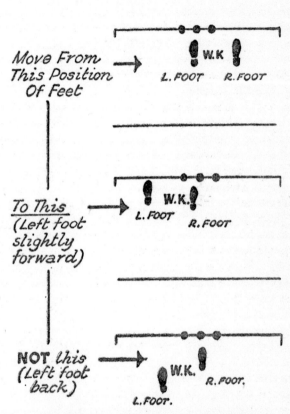

Move From
This Position
Of Feet →   W.K
          L. FOOT   R. FOOT

To This →   W.K.
(Left foot   L. FOOT   R. FOOT
slightly
forward)

NOT this →   W.K.   R. FOOT.
(Left foot
back)   L. FOOT.

Diagram Showing Correct And
Incorrect Movements of The
Wicket Keeper (W.K.) When
Taking A Leg Break.

DIAGRAM XII

go out to meet the ball. It is quite possible that he will do neither; but the added confidence makes him bat better in every way. You want the reverse. Your wish is that his fear of being stumped will cramp his style. In any case stumping is such fun, and you need to get practice at it; so my advice is to stand up to the wicket unless the bowler is fast or the wicket really bumpy.

And if you stand up stand *right up*. It is no harder to keep wicket standing close enough to stump than it is to stand a yard back. That is useless. Remember that some part of the batsman's foot (or bat) must be *touching the ground* behind the crease. However much of his foot there may be behind the crease it is no good to him if it is in the air. He is out—"stumped", and he is also out if his toe or the side of his boot is *on* the line only.

You must keep your eyes on the ball as it comes to you; but keep "half an eye" on the batsman's feet. If you see a chance, whip off the bails; but do not do so un-necessarily just to show how smart you are, as this wastes time and annoys the umpire. You should, however, always have the feeling of being *ready* to break the wicket every time you take the ball.

You will remember that I said that you must not play across the flight of the ball with your hands any more than you should with your bat. As with every rule there are exceptions. A batsman plays across the line of the ball when he makes a perfectly correct hook stroke. The exception in the case of the wicket-keeper is when he is taking the bowling of a slow bowler (probably bowling breaks) and the batsman gives hope that he may offer a chance of being stumped. The signs are more favourable if the batsman plays forward at full stretch than if he moves out of his ground to meet the ball.

If you see the batsman scraping forward, you must take the slight risk of moving your hands across the line by taking them further to the off or leg, as the case may be, and sweeping them towards the wicket, gathering the ball on the way. The risk is, of course, that by moving the hands across the line of flight you may miss the ball and give away a bye. But it is worth it; and presently the batsman will reach a shade too far forward, so that he raises his toe or drags it over for a fraction of a second. You alter the sweep of your hands just enough to flick off a bail, and out goes the batsman.

The quickest movement for balls which come just over the top of the stumps or just to the side of them, when the batsman offers a chance of stumping, is a kind of *punching* movement made by straightening the elbows. Try it.

CATCHES

When you are standing up to the wicket most catches are a matter of luck—provided that you would have taken the ball correctly if the batsman had not touched it. Your hands are waiting for the ball, and the distance between the bat and your gloves is so small and the time taken for the ball to travel that distance so short that you have no chance to move your hands. If the bat has barely touched the ball, the course of the ball will hardly alter, and you will take the catch. On the contrary, a real snick will cause such a change of direction that a catch is not a possibility to the keeper. I have even heard it said that "if the spectators can hear a missed chance at the wicket it is not a missed chance at the wicket". Can you work that out?

It is a different matter when you are standing back to a fast or fast-medium bowler. The question is—how far back? The answer is—far enough back for the average ball of that particular bowler on that particular wicket to come to you at the easiest possible height. The easiest possible height is when the ball has dropped from its bounce to just below the level of your waist. There will, of course, be many balls which are not average. To those which reach you chest-high you should move slightly to the side to take; and to those which are dropping earlier you should take a pace forward with one foot.

In my view, the stance should be different for standing back. When standing "up" the footwork takes place before or as the ball pitches. When standing back to a fast bowler it takes place as the ball passes the batsman, for he may deflect it. You are really a glorified slip or fine-leg. Glorified, because you have some nice big gloves with which to help you catch the balls. There is neither need to crouch so low nor, do I think, ought you to stand so flat-footed. Your heels will still be on the ground but your weight should be forward on your toes to enable you to spring or dive right or left at the greatest possible speed. I do not know whether Col. S. C. Griffith, the Sussex and England player, would agree with this, but the almost miraculous catches I saw him make at Manchester in the "Victory Test" against the Australians suggested spring off the toes to me.

If you are standing back you must, of course, sprint up to the wicket every time the batsman hits the ball (unless it has been fielded by one of the close-in players) to be ready to receive the fieldsman's throw in.

APPEALING

When you appeal, for goodness' sake do so in a firm way. Many boys seem shy of doing this, and it makes an awkward position for the umpire. I have often suffered in this connection, when umpiring school matches, as I am slightly deaf. I know that an umpire should not be slightly deaf, but there it is—I am and I cannot help it!

What is the poor umpire to do in the following case, which is a many times true story in my experience? The batsman misses the ball with both feet out of his ground but, almost instantaneously, grounds his bat behind the crease. The wicket-keeper also misses the ball with his hands but it bounces on to the stumps from his pad, and a bail falls. No sound is heard, but the keeper turns his face towards me at the square-leg umpire's position and opens his mouth. I have, meanwhile, decided that the batsman grounded his bat after the bail was dislodged and that he was, therefore, clearly "out".

What am I to do? I cannot give a decision unless appealed to. Does the fact that the wicket-keeper is looking at me with his mouth open mean that he has appealed; or is it just that he has adenoids and likes looking at me anyway? The rule of cricket is that an appeal may be made at any time until the next ball is bowled. If I enquire "Did anyone appeal?" and there had, in fact, been no appeal, some less obtuse member of the side may say "How *was* it?" I should have to give the batsman "out" in answer to an appeal which would not have been made unless I had spoken.

If I do not make that enquiry there may be an awkward pause, with half the side giving me puzzled and even hurt glances. The only answer that I know to this problem is that the wicket-keeper, or anyone else who is in a good position to see, should appeal in a clear and audible voice. And it is more important that it should be audible than clear. If I hear a large noise which sounds rather like "S A T"? I shall not think that the keeper is asking me the aorist tense of the verb "to sit", but that he is enquiring whether the batsman is out.

Do not appeal unnecessarily, but be sure to appeal if

you are in doubt. It is for the umpire to give the batsman the benefit of the doubt—not you.

It often happens that the wicket-keeper is in a better position than is the bowler to appeal for l.b.w. decisions. If the bowler is a good one he has followed through to the off side of the wicket, and from where he is, the batsman's legs look clear of the leg stump. From your position, directly behind the wicket, you can see perfectly that the leg which the ball hit is covering the leg-stump. You must, therefore, appeal without waiting to see whether the bowler does so or not. If you think the batsman was out then appeal straight away clearly and loudly, but not in an aggressive or bullying manner. Umpires are human, even if masters, and do not like to be bullied.

One more thing (and this applies equally to batsmen) —if the appeal goes against you, do not show your disappointment by so much as a flicker on your face or by any movement of annoyance. Nothing looks worse than any questioning of a decision. Sometimes an umpire may give a decision which seems to everyone on the field to be wrong, and which may, in fact, be wrong.

Let us suppose that the ball had been played quite hard by the bat on to the batsman's pad when he would otherwise have been clearly l.b.w. The bowler had inadvertently appealed and the umpire had raised his finger. If that batsman, knowing quite well that he is not out, cheerfully turns towards the pavilion without a sign of surprise, disagreement or annoyance, then I say the cricket has been raised to the level of Cricket with a big C and he has earned, and will get from those who understand, more admiration than if he had made a century.

Inside himself he will be very disappointed, but as he takes off his pads, he will be wise if he reflects that "it all comes out in the wash" and that, a fortnight ago the umpire (possibly the same one) had given him "not out" for a catch at the wicket when he actually had felt the ball just touch his batting glove.

TAKING RETURNS

By no means the least important part of the keeper's work is the smart taking of fielders' return throws. He should, of course, station himself close up to the wicket, which must be directly between him and the thrower. There is no trouble with the throws which come in as they should, full pitch or long hop over the stumps; but many do not. The keeper should do his best to take the wide ones by moving one foot only. The other foot, being in its original position, will then form a kind of guide to the wicket, which must be put down with the same sort of sweep as is used for stumping. The wicket should be put down by the punching movement when the ball comes really close to it.

Many fielders have the annoying habit of throwing half-volleys, or worse still, just short of half-volleys. This happens because they aim at the stumps instead of a little above them or else well short. If the throw is straight, the ball will hit the stumps near the bottom and no harm is done. The batsman may even be run out, but it is still a bad throw.

When the ball is coming in on the right and looks like pitching about three or four feet short, the keeper should put his left foot where his right was (forming a new anchor) and take a step forward with his right leg so that he can gather the ball immediately after it has pitched. Similar balls to the left should be dealt with by putting the right foot where the left was, and taking a pace forward with the left. Without changing the positions of the feet, the keeper cannot step forward because the stumps would be in the way. There will be many balls so badly thrown in that the only thing to do is to stop them; and no blame will attach to the keeper for failing to run out the batsman.

GLOVES

These should be well padded, with thimbles in the finger-tips, and must be a loose fit though not sloppy. Gloves on the tight side, which seem possible when you first go out, soon become impossible; for your hands swell from taking ball after ball and as you get hot. An inner pair of chamois leather gloves is a good thing to have.

CHAPTER VI

CAPTAINCY

YOUR job as captain is tremendously important. You probably follow County Cricket in the papers, and watch it when you get an opportunity. You will have realized that even in this class of cricket, where most of the players are professionals or amateurs of much experience, the quality of the captain has a very great effect on the standard and performance of the County XI.

Frequently a county which has had poor results for years will make a big advance under a new and enthusiastic captain. If this is true in the case of experienced players how much the more important is the character, skill and knowledge of the captain in a Prep. School XI, composed of boys who have nearly everything to learn.

The qualities desirable in the personalities of the captains of county and Prep. School XI's are much the same; but the problems they have to face are very different. In this and the following chapter, captaincy only as it applies to Prep. School cricket will be discussed, though club captains may find some helpful hints.

Most important of all is the spirit of the game. You must feel this spirit yourself, and it will communicate itself to the other members of the team. The winning of the match should be the *most* important and the *least* important consideration. How can that curious contradiction be true? A few examples will make my meaning clear.

(1) Your side has made 170 and you have taken 9 wickets of your opponents XI for 42 runs. There are only a few minutes left for play. It is most important to get the

last man out in those few minutes to win the match. Not a second must be lost in slovenly changing of places at the end of the over. The last batsman arrives. He is a very small boy, terribly nervous and white-faced, perhaps playing in his first match. As he arrives at the wicket you hear him say to his master who is umpiring, "Oh, sir, I have brought the wrong bat!" True enough, in his fluster he has picked up a bat about three sizes too big for him. You tell the umpire that you are willing for him to change it. The master calls out to the players in the pavilion—"send out a small bat". The little boy runs towards the pavilion to meet the boy who is running out with another bat but a whole precious minute has been wasted. Wasted? NO!

(2) The other side made 170. You have lost 9 wickets for 42. There are only a few minutes to go. The most important thing, so that you can make a draw of it instead of losing, is that your last man should not get out; but he is a very poor bat. The boy who has just returned to the pavilion was run out off the first ball of the over and a safe but stodgy man will have to deal with the remaining five balls. There may or may not be time for another over. It depends upon how long your last man takes to get to the wicket. He starts out at a very slow pace, either because he has not fully realized the position or because he thinks that is the right thing to do for his side. You, as captain, call out to him—"Buck up, young Smith, get a move on!" He walks briskly to the wicket. The stodgy boy safely survives the five balls and there is *just* time to start a new over. Off the fourth ball your No. 11 is bowled and the match is lost. What a pity he had not taken longer to walk to the wicket? Surely not!

(3) You have got your opponents on the run. Your bowlers are hostile, your fielders are on their toes and are fielding in the most aggressive manner. You are keyed up

to maintain the pressure in every way. It is most important that there should be no slackening or easing of the atmosphere. A fastish good length ball pops up and hits the batsman a nasty crack on the head. You come forward to help him. He is brave and tries to take his stance—you tell him to take his time, but he says he is all right. His eyes are fuzzy with unshed tears and he puts his bat in his left-handed partner's middle-and-leg blockhole, so that his pads are practically covering the stumps. Your wicket-keeper says—"You've got the wrong guard," and you look approvingly at that wicket-keeper.

(4) Their last man is in and they need only five to win. The bowler sends down a long hop which the batsman well and truly hooks. Your square-leg sprints ten yards and brings off a really wonderful one-handed catch. "Oh, well caught, Brown," you yell, and your opponents in the pavilion give him a burst of clapping and cheering. But what is this? Brown is making the wash-out sign with his arms and calls out to the umpire—"My feet were over the line, sir" (a recent heavy shower had made the boundary line too faint for the umpire to see it against the evening sun). The umpire signals a six. You and your team clap vigorously and cheerfully.

Leaving particular examples, we may say that the true spirit of cricket is expressed by the will to win and intense hostility (within the limits of fairness and courtesy) until the last ball is bowled. From that moment, win or lose or draw, the hostility is dropped and friendship, appreciation and good fellowship take its place.

If you have read such historical novels as *Ivanhoe*, *Sir Nigel* or *The White Company*, you will remember that in the Age of Chivalry the Knights would have a good dinner together, before going out to a jousting or "very pleasant and profitable encounter", where they would do their best to kill one another. Then, if they were not too severely wounded to walk they would meet in the evening for a jolly good banquet. There is not very much of that spirit left in the modern world, but it can, and does, survive on the cricket field. Long may it do so; and my hope is that you will help to keep it alive and flourishing.

PICKING THE TEAM

In some schools the master picks the team, but in most, I think, there is a selection committee with the master as chairman and advisor. I am sure that this is the better way. The discussions during the meeting are often of great value, and each member, including the master, may learn something new. In my own school we have on the committee the captain, vice-captain and one or more of the experienced members of the regular team. As chairman of such committees, I have found you boys always to be fair but not always wise. You will vote against your best friends or even yourselves, if out of form. This is as it should be; but where you are not wise is that you are too inclined to consider the candidates for places in the XI on their merits as cricketers rather than as to how they will fit together to form a balanced team.

Provided that you have four really good bowlers of different types, the bowling ability of anyone else need not be considered (unless other things are equal). You will need some batsmen who are safe, and some who can score fast. You must have the very best wicket-keeper in the school, however bad he may be as a bat. He will be more valuable to the side than the next best wicket-keeper who is also a good bat. Your fielders also must be balanced. It would obviously be a poor fielding side which contained ten superb slip fielders who could not throw!

In my experience of many years as a Prep. School-master the first seven or eight boys practically pick themselves. It is the last three or four who give the trouble. There generally seem to be about a dozen boys to be considered for those last three or four places. It is important, therefore, that you, as captain, should have very clear ideas about your seven or eight automatic choices.

What are their positions in the batting order? From the batting point of view do you want more safety or more run-getting possibilities?

Have you got your four good bowlers of varying types?

Perhaps more important than either of these questions is the matter of fielding. In what positions do your seven or eight field best? When you have decided this you follow up with the question as to which fielding positions are still left to be filled, and which of the candidates will best fill those places.

You will not select any boy, however good, if he is not keen or if he does not play the game in the right spirit.

PRELIMINARIES

Be sure that you and your vice-captain are ready to receive your guests, if it is a home match. You first greet their master, who introduces his own captain to you. Having shown him and his team their changing room, you should invite him to toss before he changes, so that you will have longer to write your batting order and to see your openers padded up if your side is batting.

As home captain you will do the tossing. Let this be no sordid business with a penny in the pavilion, but let it be a fine affair—a fitting prelude to the match. Go right out on to the field and fling the half-crown high and fast-spinning.

Let us suppose your opponent calls wrongly, and you have to decide whether or not to bat first. Many matters must be considered, or rather, should have been considered in advance, but one thing definitely *should not* be taken into account. I refer to the common wish of your team to put in the other side because of nervousness. Every time a fear is given way to this makes it stronger for next time, but every time that fear is mastered *you* become stronger until the fear is defeated. Normally the thing to do is to bat first for two main reasons:

(1) Your side will get the best of the wicket.

(2) Your side can take its time in scoring, and unless you are all out, you can choose the moment for a declaration.

You will generally (after taking into consideration the tea interval) divide the playing time into two equal parts to decide when half-time is. Then you should bat a little past that time so that the other side will have to hurry the score along a shade faster than you did—if it is to win. Hurry may mean mistakes; and mistakes may mean wickets falling; and wickets falling may mean victory for your side. Of course, if your batsmen have been very slow you will have to go on well past the half-way, with the consequent danger of your bowlers having insufficient time to get all the other side out.

Most Prep. School matches are from 2 p.m. to 6.30 p.m. The tea interval often takes up half an hour. This leaves four hours actual playing time. If you let your side bat for 2¼ hours and they have scored at the rate of 60 runs per hour your total will be 135. To get the 136 runs necessary to win, allowing for the interval between the innings, the other side will have to score at the rate of 85 runs per hour. This is not an unreasonable thing to ask them to do, but it will probably entail their taking some risks.

It is, of course, difficult to say what is the normal rate of scoring, as grounds vary so much in size, and the presence or absence of spectators to throw back the ball from boundary hits makes a big difference. All such matters must be taken into account when trying to find the ideal moment to declare.

There are times, however, when it is wise to make the other side bat first. The most usual reason is that the wicket is inclined to be sticky. There may have been rain early on followed by hot sun without much wind. The wicket may be difficult at first, but a fresh breeze just springing up makes you think that it will play more easily later on. Obviously they go in.

In showery weather, when the showers are far enough apart for the grass to dry between them, if the start of the match takes place during a dry period, it may well pay to let your bowlers have the use of the new, dry and shiny ball. You hope that your innings will start just after a shower. You would, of course, see that their bowlers had piles of sawdust to help them. Even so the wet ball is a handicap to them and the wet ground is more difficult for their fielders—especially if any of them is fool enough to be wearing rubber-soled shoes.

In poor weather, you may be able to start a match though the clouds look so threatening that you fear you will not get in a full game. In such cases, when you are playing against a side which you think is likely to be weak in batting, it is well to put them in. They may be all out in an hour, and you may be able to get the necessary runs in three-quarters of an hour just before rain stops play for the day. Yet you would not have been able to declare, if you had gone in first, after batting for only three-

PLATES 9 and 10. These two pictures must be carefully compared. A ball has been rolled along the mat to show how one bad fault can cause others and make you miss the ball, probably to be bowled. Carefully observe the right foot. In Plate 9 the batsman *has allowed his right foot to turn until the instep is facing down the wicket*. This has caused much trouble. It has allowed his hips and shoulders to turn until they nearly face the bowler and this has moved the whole bat an inch or two to the leg side. His bat is travelling up the white line between L and M, but the ball is well to the off of that line and is missed.

PLATE 10, on the other hand, shows the right foot parallel to the crease *until the ball has been hit*. This has kept hips and shoulders sideways on to the bowler, resulting in a true movement of the bat down the line of the ball. These two pictures are most important.

quarters of an hour. You would have had to bat for the full hour and three-quarters. They would not have had a knock, and the game would have been a draw.

Make sure that you fully understand the rules for a one-day match, which are explained in detail in Part II, Chapter 2 of this book.

THE BATTING ORDER

A good start is of great importance. It gives confidence to the remainder of the side, and it prevents the opponents from having that winning feeling which gives them an extra bit of power. You must therefore start with two sound bats, and all the better if one of them is a left-hander. This makes it harder for the bowlers immediately to find a length and direction.

In any case try to find two batsmen whose styles are different, so that the same ball would not be of good length to each of them. But they must be sound. One may be rather sticky and stodgy (provided he knows when to hit out or get out) but the other must be capable of pushing along the score at a reasonable rate.

No. 3 is generally your star batsman. He does not go in first because he can get on better with his brilliant scoring strokes if the openers have taken the shine off the ball, and, perhaps, the first sting and fury of the fast bowler.

No. 4 is a most important position. The batsman for this job is one who is capable of two entirely different games. Sometimes he has to come in to "stop the rot", when the first two wickets have fallen very quickly with scarcely any runs on the board. He must therefore be a good man at pure defence until the situation has improved.

F

At other times, when the opening pair has given the side a good but rather slow start, and No. 3's stay has not been very long, he may find himself partnering the stodgy opener. He will then be expected to take the place of No. 3 and produce plenty of scoring shots.

Therefore you should put one of your best and most experienced cricketers at No. 4. If you are the right type of batsman it is a very good place for you yourself to fill, as the game may be at the stage when your wise control can be of great value.

No. 5 may well be a really good bat though he is not so safe as the earlier men; and No. 6 should be a stout defender to partner him or the big hitter who comes in at No. 7. Nos. 8, 9 and 10 will be what they happen to be, but No. 11 should not necessarily consider himself the worst bat of the side. No. 3 may still be there, or the big-hitting No. 7, so he should have some defence and be a good runner, able to help in farming the bowling as explained in chapter 2.

You will also have to take your bowlers into account. It would be better for your opening bowlers to go in Nos. 8 and 9 than 10 and 11, so that they may have some rest between batting and bowling. You must be prepared to vary this order if the state of the game makes defence or attack, as the case may be, of greater importance.

Give your batsmen advice when quick runs are necessary. Tell them that much time is wasted whenever a wicket falls, and that they should therefore take a few minutes to get used to the light, pace of the pitch, etc., before hitting out too freely. If there is a clock in view, tell them at what rate it is necessary for them to score, and that 6 runs average per over is about 120 runs per hour—mighty fast scoring.

If A has banged three balls in one over to the boundary, from the weak bowler, it is quite in order for B then to play a maiden over from the accurate bowler the other end.

When there is no clock visible from the ground the captain *must* have a watch. The moment for a declaration is so vital (the fact that poor young Jones is now 49 not out has nothing to do with it!) and his instructions to the in-going batsmen are so important, that the captain must know much more than roughly what the time is. The two umpires should have made sure that their watches were exactly the same, and the captain have been "in on this" too and be certain that his own agrees with theirs.

As captain you are responsible for the behaviour of your side in the pavilion, and by your keenness and your authority you must see to it that the members of your team follow the game and give encouragement to the batsmen by their cheers. I have known it to happen (sometimes in my own school, to my shame be it said), that a young batsman has batted pluckily at a crisis and has hit a lovely four, when every run was needed, without any indication from the pavilion that his stroke has been observed or, more important, that his team is *with* him in his great efforts to meet the situation. You must firmly squash any ragging about. "Boys will be boys" is all very well; but if they are cricketers enough to be chosen for the XI they must be cricketers in the pavilion as well as on the field.

Often the pavilion is in line with the wickets. In such a case you must be very careful to see that there is no moving about behind the bowler's arm when the bowling is from the pavilion end. Any necessary movement can take place when the wicket-keeper is at that end. You should also chase, or cause to be chased, any members of the school who wander about behind the bowler's arm at either end. I am afraid I can give you no advice as to what to do if the culprits are "parents"—except to ask your headmaster to deal with the situation and he will probably not know what to do! Of course if they are your own parents you will know how to act without any advice from me.

CHAPTER VII

CAPTAINCY (*Continued*)

CRICKET is a game of beauty and order and dis-
cipline. Nothing looks less like beauty and order than
the sight of some half-dozen or more of the fielding side
going out to the wicket in advance of the umpires.

The proper start to a match or an innings is surely
this. The umpires leave the pavilion, walk to the wickets
and place the bails in position. The setting of the bails
is a sign that the game has begun and you, as captain of
the fielding side, *at once* lead your team on to the field.
You have previously told your opening bowlers which
end they are bowling and which one is starting. Your
fielders also know this and their positions to each bowler,
so there is no fuss and bother upon arrival. Each boy
goes to his place. You will probably wave to this one and
that to change his position slightly but that is all.

You will have trained them to keep an eye on you
throughout the game so that you can move them at any
time without having to shout at them.

As the fielding side reaches the middle the opening
batsmen leave the pavilion, arrive at the wickets and one
takes his guard. Should he turn out to be a left-hander
the fieldsmen will alter their positions without a word
from you *for you have given them instructions in advance*. The
batsman glances round the ground in order to take a
mental photograph of the placing of the field, then
settles himself to his stance. The umpire calls "Play!"
and the match, with all its thrilling possibilities, has
begun in real earnest.

The batsman has had a glance round the positions of

the fielders. Let us now do the same. What are these positions? In books on cricket you will often find excellent diagrams of suitable field placings for the various types of bowling such as fast, out-swingers, in-swingers, off-breaks over the wicket, off-breaks round the wicket, slow left arm, leg-breaks, and so on. I do not think that these diagrams will be of much use to you because your bowlers will not be accurate enough. The county captain and bowler set a field and the bowler bowls to it—or should. Some Prep. School bowlers are remarkably good, but in general, *any* ball may come down at any moment.

What you need is a "general purpose" field setting. If you have extra good bowlers your team is probably extra good, and you would not be its captain unless you were yourself an exceptionally good cricketer. If so, you will know how to modify my suggested placings and even to use the positions shown in the cricket books for various types of bowling. But if you, who are now reading this book, are an ordinary captain of an ordinary Prep. School side, I think you will find the general purpose field will keep down the runs made by your opponents.

Before discussing the diagram I must mention the question of long-stop or no long-stop. Unless you have an unusually good wicket-keeper and accurate bowlers, you will find it is well worth while having one, except to the slowest bowlers. He will probably save a dozen or fifteen byes in an innings, and it is extremely doubtful if his presence in some other position would save more than four or five runs. Apart from the byes saved, the wicket-keeper is much more likely to get a man stumped if he knows that his possible missing of the ball will not automatically score a bye for the other side.

The principle of the field placings shown in the diagram opposite is not a new one. It is called the "inner

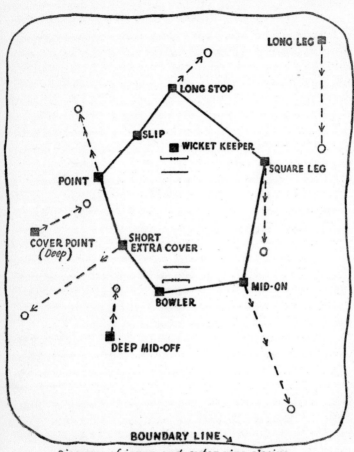

Diagram of inner and outer ring placing.
"General Purpose" field setting.

DIAGRAM X

and outer ring". The idea is that the inner ring should save singles, whilst the outer ring prevents fours.

The squares and BLOCK LETTERS indicate the general purpose field. Long-stop, slip, backward point, short extra-cover, bowler, mid-on and square-leg form the inner ring and should be near enough to save the singles. Long-leg, deep cover and deep mid-off form the outer ring to save the fours. Mid-off appears to be in a betwixt-and-between position, but this is intentional. So many balls are firmly hit past the bowler that he must be close enough to prevent hard hit singles. (Short extra-cover will avoid singles from gently hit balls in that direction.) At the same time mid-off is deep enough to cover a large area for the purpose of saving fours.

Be sure that the men you place in the outer ring are really deep—generally on the boundary. It is quite astonishing how hard it is to make boys stay right out. They edge in all the time, and must be watched.

Obviously you cannot save all the singles and all the fours; or the other side would not score at all, would it? You cannot prevent scoring (and it would not be much of a match if you did), but your object is to cut it down. Now if a big-hitting batsman—particularly of the cross-bat variety—comes in, the field will have to be changed. The arrows are suggestions as to the changes that the fielders should make, and the circles show their new positions. Long-leg moves to the square-leg boundary, and mid-on to long-on. Square-leg will try to save singles on the "on" side by shifting more towards mid-on. Mid-off comes up to save singles; and short extra-cover drops back to the boundary to save fours. Cover comes up to the normal position. Point goes deeper and finer for the mishits. Long-stop moves to very fine leg. You still have inner and outer rings of the same numbers, but in different positions.

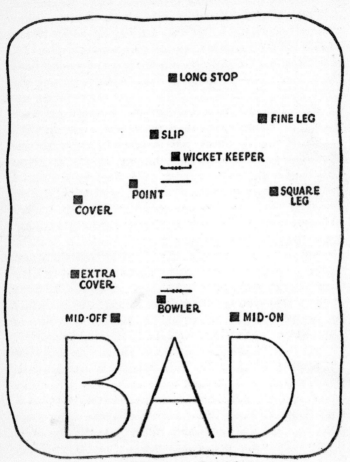

A very bad placing of field
DIAGRAM XI

The very worst placing of the field, and it is often seen in Prep. School cricket, is that which satisfies neither purpose. Most of the fielders are too far away to save singles yet they are too close to cover enough ground to prevent fours. On page 89 is a diagram of a very badly placed field. How I should like to be batting; wouldn't you?

Having placed your field suitably you will get better results by encouragement than by crossness during a match. When Robinson has dropped a catch, do you think he is more likely to hold the next one if you call out "You blithering ass!" or even "Oh *Rob*inson!", than if you say "Oh, hard luck, Robinson—well tried!", however easy the catch was and however futile his attempt may have been? This will not prevent your giving him some extra fielding practice next day if he is keen, or dropping him from the side if he is lazy or if there is a more worthy substitute. There is one job the boy captain often forgets to do, and that is to call *loudly* and *early* the name of the fielder who should try for the catch when he sees two or more boys running for the same ball. Many an easy chance is missed through the fielders colliding.

You will remember reading about "farming the bowling" in Chapter II. Your opponents may try this; and you must be up to their tricks so that you can scheme in the opposite direction. Their good batsman wants to score fours or twos. You should withdraw your inner ring. This will not only tempt him to take a single when he thinks it would look so silly not to do so, but will also make it so much harder for him to get the ball past the fieldsmen for his twos and fours. *Count* the balls of the over, and on the fifth ball bring in your fielders extra close. He is going to try for a quick single that ball or the next. If he fails to do so, your men must start close in during the next over when the bad batsman is taking the bowling. He wants a single—desperately. You must prevent this if it is at all possible.

Whilst on the subject of having the field arranged differently for the two batsmen, I must urge you never to hesitate to tell a fielder to take up one position to one of the batsmen, but a different place to the other. An obvious example is that to have a silly mid-off or forward short-leg may be wise when batsman A is striking, whereas these positions would be unsuitable, or even dangerous, when batsman B faces the bowling.

On those occasions when the other side has batted first and you realize that there is little or no chance of getting them all out, you must put yourself into the position of the opposing captain and try to guess his plans with regard to a declaration. Here is another example of the importance of your watch, if no clock is visible. Try to decide what he wants his batsmen to do; then do your best to frustrate his designs. If he has several wickets in hand but wants some quick runs, you should set your field more with the idea of saving runs than of getting wickets. Every game is different and offers fresh problems. Your cricket brain will have plenty to do.

Train your fielders to return the ball to the bowler as an easy catch. The effort of stooping to pick up a ball, rolled along the ground, is tiring for the bowler and reduces his effectiveness. At the same time avoid that stupid practice, which is creeping into cricket, of throwing the ball from fielder to fielder on a sort of Cook's tour on its way to the bowler. The wicket-keeper, if he is standing back, may throw to slip, point or short-leg and he to the bowler or mid-off.

One final piece of advice before we pass on to another subject—beware of a great danger to your team's success which crops up from time to time. I refer to those occasions upon which everything seems to go almost too well at first. Your bowlers are in fine form; catches go straight to fielders and are held; throws hit, instead of just miss, the stumps. Wicket after wicket falls for scarcely any runs. All their best bats have gone. BEWARE! There may occur an unconscious slackening of effort on the part of your bowlers and fielders. You yourself may even relax and let your mind dwell on the possibility of making an experiment with the batting order. On such occasions a stubborn stand is apt to occur. At first no one takes much notice. Suddenly you realize that 23 for 7 has become 56 for 7. This won't do! You call back your powers of concentration, you brace your team, you change your tactics. It is of no avail. Now, balls just miss wickets, catches go out of reach, an easy chance is dropped, bowlers and fielders get flustered, the batsmen, realizing that they are living in fairyland, bang the ball about all over the place. Ninety for 7; 100 for 7; 120 for 7; it is ridiculous, but it is true.

I cannot tell you what to do, because nothing seems to work at this stage; but I *can* tell you that if there had not been that almost imperceptible easing off an hour ago, you would probably have had them all out for under 40. So beware! In 1946 the Indians, C. T. Sarwate and S. Bannerjee, playing against Surrey, scored 249 in a *tenth wicket stand*. You never know in cricket. No match is won until it is won; or lost until it is lost.

The match against the Somerset Stragglers, mentioned in the Introduction to Part II in connection with Arthur Newton's performance, is a good example of this. As I am writing from memory my figures may not be absolutely correct, but I am sure that they are very nearly right. The Stragglers, batting first, made 270. This seemed a reasonable score, but caused us no uneasiness as we had a very strong batting side. However, we were outed for 103; and, following on, we had lost two of our best batsmen for 18 in the second innings at close of play on the first day. The remaining eight wickets had still to make 150 runs before the Stragglers would have to bat again; and then they would have all the ten wickets of their second innings to make any few necessary runs to win. Could any match be more certainly lost?

Yet, next day, we were able to *declare* at 379 for 7 (mainly through the grand batting of A. G. Marshall and H. D. King); and we got their last man out in the last over of the match with their second innings total only about 90. This gave us a win with some 80 runs to spare, and I think it was about the most thrilling match in which I ever played.

To return to your duties as captain. These do not finish with the match. The moment stumps are drawn you are again the host. You give the visiting side three cheers, look after their comfort and see them off. Try to arrange that all the members of your side are present as the other school drives away. In a boarding school this is automatic; but in a day school some of the boys may have a long distance to travel, or parents may have come to fetch them. It may be difficult, or even impossible, but do try.

CHAPTER VIII

WATCHING TEST AND COUNTY CRICKET

WHEN you go to watch a Test or County match really *three* of you go. *You* as a lover of cricket; *You* as a present or future captain; *You* as a batsman, bowler, fielder or wicket-keeper. The first wishes to see the game as a whole and to enjoy its beauty; the second tries to realize what the captain is thinking, why he has changed the bowling, why he has shifted the fielders, why he has not put Blank on to bowl, why he has left such a large gap between the fielders in a certain part of the ground although the batsman has already hit two boundaries through that gap—and so on. The third is concerned, as the case may be, with the footwork of the batsman, the action of the bowler, the way the fielder picks up and throws or the wicket-keeper's method of dealing with leg-balls.

Now the first has by far the easiest job, and I think he should have a jolly good innings; but you must be careful or you will find that No. 2 has not had much chance, and No. 3 has not even had a look in during the day. Nos 1 and 2 can be combined to a certain extent, but No. 3 cuts them out. When he is busy the others may miss thrilling strokes or balls or catches. But if you are to get full value from your day, you must spend part of the time studying the *methods* of the first-class cricketers you are watching.

It is most important, however, to observe very closely and accurately, or you may get entirely wrong ideas. You will remember that I recommend the back of the left hand to be towards mid-off or extra-cover. I had been teaching this to my boys some years ago, maintaining that no first-class batsman had the back of his left hand really facing the bowler in the way a few of them held their bats. Well—I took some of them with me to Lord's, and there was Bruce Mitchell batting magnificently for South Africa against England. Suddenly one of the boys exclaimed, "Oh, sir, Mitchell has the back of his left hand the way you say is wrong." This was awkward for me, as it certainly looked as if the boy was accurate in his observation. I examined Mitchell's position very carefully through my field-glasses. It was true that as he stood there awaiting the ball the back of his left hand was facing straight forward; but, just before the bowler completed his delivery, Mitchell moved it round so that it faced in the direction of mid-off to extra-cover—my reputation was saved!

You will realize from this example how important it is to watch most carefully, and to have a pair of field-glasses. Bruce Mitchell made a century in that innings. I shall always remember his face, as I saw it through my glasses, when he was waiting for the ball to be bowled. I never saw, before or since, an expression which so remarkably combined intense concentration and watchfulness with absolute *calm*. His century certainly did not come by accident.

You must also realize that first-class cricketers do not always give perfect examples of "how it should be done". A young and agile fielder, when he chases and picks up a ball, may turn the wrong way before throwing, but so quick is he, and so hard does he throw, that he is a very valuable fielder. If, however, he had trained himself to turn the other way he would have been quicker still and still more valuable.

I want you to watch for these faults without losing

your admiration for these splendid young men. They have reached such a high standard that they are playing for a strong first-class county; but such faults as they have may be due to lack of tuition. Perhaps they have not had a cricket coach at all at their schools, and very likely they are better than many who have had every facility.

I wish you to become a really knowledgeable cricketer, so I again urge you to watch for such faults. BUT keep your thoughts to yourself, or share them quietly with your companion. Nothing is much more annoying than to hear criticism after criticism of the players from the "know-alls" seated round the field. Many of them have never been "in the middle" in their lives. Cricket is the easiest game in the world—from the pavilion or boundary line seats.

PLATE 11 shows the defensive forward shot to a ball just outside the off stumps. Note that the right foot is still parallel to the crease, weight is on front foot, *left knee well bent*, good position of hands, left elbow pointing at bowler, right arm ready to join left in a powerful push, ball is being played opposite the left leg, head down, eyes watching the ball right on to the bat.

PLATE 12. This is very nearly the *finish* of an off drive, so the turning of the right foot, hips and shoulders is correct. The ball is well away, the bat is pointing straight to where the ball has gone—not dragged round to the leg side. As the batsman had to hold this tiring position while the camera was focussed, lights adjusted and a short exposure given, he cannot be blamed for certain faults. The left knee is not sufficiently bent, the body should be leaning more forward in line with the right leg and the right hand is too near the blade of the bat. If this had been close to the left hand his left arm would have been straighter.

Part II

TO MASTERS AND THEIR BOYS

INTRODUCTION

YOUNG boys do not and cannot think far ahead. A youngster with an examination in a year's time is quite happy. "There is plenty of time, sir!" What his cricket will be like at 40, 50 or 60 is nothing to him; but surely it is our job, as schoolmasters, to think ahead for him.

Let us call to mind Lord Ebbisham and "Billy" Williams taking 100 wickets each in good cricket at the age of seventy, of Stanley Colman at about that age skippering The Wanderers and offering an impregnable defence at No. 11 and foiling the exuberant near-victors. Playing against the Somerset Stragglers, in a two-day match, I was amazed to find the old Somerset wicket-keeper, Arthur Newton, "keeping" quite up to first-class standard at the age of 73. He brought off two good stumpings (one on the leg side) and held two catches in that match. The second catch was astounding, as he was standing right up to the wicket and took a veritable leg glance of J. H. Cameron's. When he was 84 Arthur Newton bought himself a new pair of wicket-keeping gloves!

Turning to less extreme ages and to the highest company, we may think of J. B. Hobbs' superb double century at the Oval against the West Indians when he was forty-eight, and of F. E. Woolley's incomparable batting at the age of fifty.

Let us think on these things and determine to give our boys those solid foundations without which cricket longevity is so unlikely.

CHAPTER I

WINTER INSTRUCTION

I HAVE proved, over many years, the extraordinary improvement in the standard of a school's cricket that can be achieved by a very limited amount of Winter instruction. By this I do not mean Winter nets. Few schools can provide the necessary space, equipment or time for nets, but most schools have a gym. or assembly room, and that is all that is necessary.

BATTING

If the "foundations" are formed as described in Part I in the Winter, the Summer nets and games are so much the more valuable. The stance, holding and lifting of the bat, movement of the feet, etc., have, by then, all been relegated to the muscular memory, and need not be thought about. Full attention can be given by the boy to watching the ball and acquiring judgment of length and flight. The task of the coach is eased, for he will not have to explain the strokes; the boys will have learnt them in the Winter, and will know them by name.

The learning of the strokes will be made by slow-motion practice. This can be done more easily and in a far more interesting manner by the use of the numbered mat which I have devised. A diagram with dimensions (see p. 102) is given and photographs of the device in use will be observed in Plates VII and XI.

The method is as follows: After the grip, stance, etc., have been learned, the boy takes his position at the wicket and the master teaches the stroke suitable for a medium-paced well pitched up ball, pitching on, say, square 7. I must now explain that, in addition to the mat, I have an old golf club with the head cut off and a solid rubber ball fixed in its place. The master then taps the ball on the chosen square and moves it slowly in the way such a ball would go. The boy plays the appropriate stroke. All the strokes can be learned in this way.

There is, however, a final and most valuable use of the mat for boys who are sufficiently advanced. The master takes up a position as far away from the batsman as space permits and announces e.g., "The next will be a fast, rising ball pitching on square W." He gives the boy a moment to think and then goes through the motion of delivering the ball. He can then check whether the boy's reactions have been correct. The master may prefer to give an intelligent boy the job of handling the "golf club" and of going through the motion of bowling, so that he can give close attention to the batsman's movements.

Before reaching this stage, however, another valuable form of practice should be undertaken. Let a tennis or soft rubber ball be rolled along the floor to the batsman who is told to play forward or back. As the ball is only rolling he must be told which to do. This practice has several advantages. The boy learns to keep his head down, to watch the ball carefully, to put his left or right leg, as the case may be, close to the line of the ball and, *above all, to play the ball when it is opposite his leg and not in front of it.* The ball may be made to roll in the desired direction by tilting an old rain-water gutter against a chair and rolling the ball down it. In this way an exact repetition of a ball may be obtained, or alternatively, a slight alteration in the position of the top of the gutter

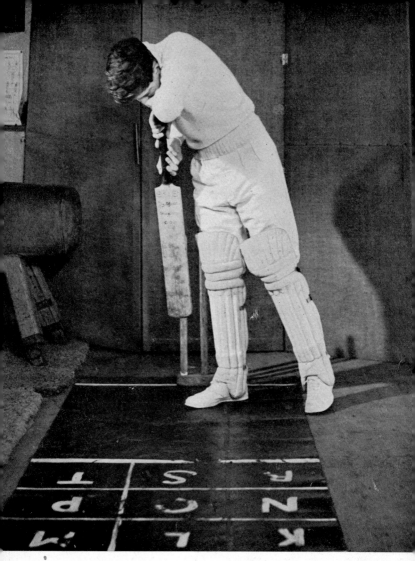

PLATE 13. This is a beautifully played back stroke. The weight is all on the right leg. The left toe is not quite touching the ground. The weight of the left leg is therefore *balancing* the weight of the head and bat. The left hand has been turned rather more away from the bowler, and the right hand, holding with fingers only, is acting as a *pusher* and a *guider*; the head is on the line of the ball, well down and nearer to the bowler than the body is. The eyes watch the ball right on to the bat; the left elbow points to the bowler, so that, in the follow-through, the bat will follow the direction the ball travels.

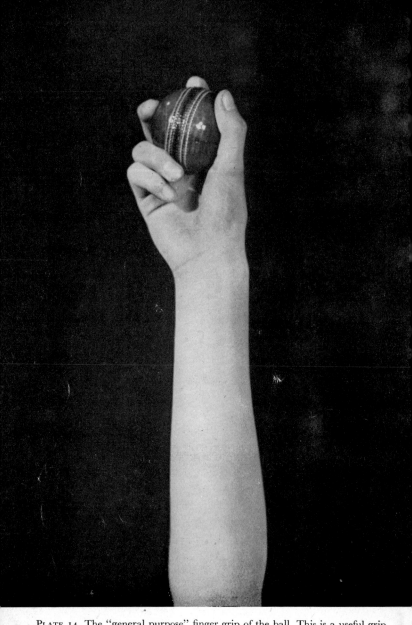

PLATE 14. The "general purpose" finger grip of the ball. This is a useful grip because, with very little alteration, it can be used for bowling off-breaks when length and direction have been mastered.

will give the ball a different direction. Boys thoroughly enjoy this practice.

It is desirable that boys should wear pads and gloves during the numbered mat practices in order to get used to their weight and "feel"; but this is not so necessary for the rolling ball practice if time is severely limited. If time is very short, pads and gloves need not be used for the mat practice until towards the end of the Easter term.

It is assumed that unless the master is an experienced player and coach he will give careful attention to Part I of this book, and carry out the tests, experiments and movements himself.

BOWLING

This does not provide so much scope for Winter practice as does batting, but considerable work of value can be undertaken. The advantage is that experiment can be carried out without having to worry about the immediate effect on the boys' bowling—a consideration which must have weight in the Summer with matches a few days ahead. There are many good books dealing with the art of bowling, but we are here trying to lay firm foundations during the Winter months. We are not concerned with the object of bowling—the dismissal of batsmen—but of teaching rhythm with the co-ordination of body, arm and wrist. The boys cannot even practise the all important "length"; but what we can do is to overhaul the mechanism, so that when the Summer term comes (or, better still, the Easter holidays) they can practise length with the most effective mechanism.

First of all, let us consider the run-up. Boys are generally very vague about this, and unless instructed,

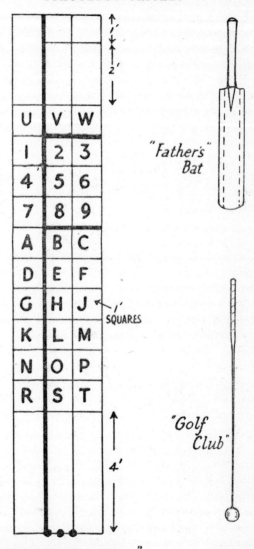

"THE NUMBERED MAT"

vary it from ball to ball. Authorities agree that the run
should be an odd number of paces, and that the left foot
should start; though they are not so clear as to whether
the left foot should start *on* the mark or *from* the mark.
Fortunately this need not worry us, for the crux of the
matter is to find the number of *bowling strides* which best
suits that particular boy, and this can be done by experiment. When the best point of departure has been thus
discovered, the run should be measured in that boy's
ordinary paces for use in making the mark. This should
be the spot from which the bowler starts his run proper,
with his left foot on the mark if he is a right-arm bowler.
He should approach the mark by one or more walking
steps. The run and delivery should be ONE-nd *bowl*: or
one, two, THREE-nd *bowl*; or one, two, three, four,
FIVE-nd *bowl*; and so on. The number in block letters
represents the jump off the left foot with the body turned
sideways to the batsman (chest facing the umpire), the
right leg passing behind the left and landing (nd) with
the foot parallel to the crease. The "*bowl*" represents the
stamping down of the left foot with *as straight a left leg as
possible*.

The right foot should be grounded as near the crease
as possible (a white chalk line on the gym. floor is essential)
and the bowling stride (*bowl*) should not be a long one. If
it is long it inevitably brings the chest facing the batsman
too soon, resulting in:

(*a*) loss of true body swing;
(*b*) low delivery;
(*c*) lack of life off the pitch.

The run-up should *not* be along a line which is an extension
of a line from wicket to wicket, but from a point to the off-
side of such a line. Furthermore, as the left foot is planted

down in the act of bowling it should be pointed towards square-leg or between square-leg and the batsman. Not straight down the wicket and, most emphatically, not towards slip. This run-up and delivery can be satisfactorily practised in the gym. When it has been mastered the next step can be taken.

The master stations himself as if he were the wicket-keeper and the boy bowls a number of imaginary balls. The master looks out for the following points (See Plate XV):

(1) Was the bowler truly sideways-on to him?

(2) Did he throw up his left arm high and straight?

(3) Was he looking at the master over his left shoulder and behind his left arm?

(4) Did the master catch a glimpse of his right hand behind his back when it was at its lowest point before swinging over?

(5) Did his left arm swing down *close* to his body?

(6) Was his right arm high at delivery?

(7) Did his right arm swing down to his left knee after delivery?

(8) Did he pivot on his left toe so that his body turned through an angle of 180°?

(9) Did he bring down his right foot after delivery, to the off-side of the wicket, thus ensuring that he had a good follow-through and was not unfairly damaging the pitch?

(10) Did he arch his body and bend backwards just before delivery?

The answer to all these questions (*except No.* 10) should be in the affirmative. If not, each point should be tackled separately, but it is probable that the correction of one fault will cure others as well, e.g. No. 5. If the bowler's left arm swung away from his body probably No. 6 was thereby affected, giving him a low delivery, as well as No. 1, bringing him chest-on to the observer. If No. 5 is corrected it will usually be found that Nos. 1 and 6 need no further attention. The answer to No. 10 should be in the negative.

Finally, the master should place himself level with the crease, as if he were at mid-on, and look for these points:

(1) Was the right foot near to, and parallel with, the crease?
(2) Was the right leg bent?
(3) Was the vertical axis of the bowler tilted away from the batsman when the left leg was in the air?
(4) When the left foot came down was the left leg straight?
(5) Was the wrist flexed backwards at the bottom of the right arm's swing so that its action was added to that of arm and body?

The answers to these questions should all be in the affirmative.

It is appreciated that no master will have the time to go through this extensive drill with more than one or two boys; but if he picks an intelligent bowler for the work, this boy can assist by carrying out the drill with another, and so on. Several sets can be working at this in the gym. simultaneously.

FIELDING

In Part I you will have read of my idea for the teaching of the correct "give". The Winter offers a good opportunity for this to be explained and practised.

Moreover, the boys can do this in pairs without supervision.

I consider it important that the master should have

practised catching without closing the hands, each hand separately and together, and also catching the ball on the blade of the bat. This is a rather striking demonstration, which brings home the point to the boys better than any amount of explanation, and if the master is still an active cricketer, I will wager his own fielding will benefit. Other work which can profitably be undertaken indoors is the running-in to the slowly rolling ball and quickly flicking it in, underhand, full pitch to the wicket-keeper just above the stumps. The chasing of the rolling ball, picking it up level with the right foot, turning *to the left* and throwing-in can also be practised.

WICKET-KEEPING

The exercise on "give" will be valuable to the wicket-keeper, but in addition, if the gym. floor is of a suitable kind, solid rubber balls can be bowled at him. For this work, as well as for the fielding practice, three old stumps stuck into a block of wood should be provided, and if another boy will oblige by standing in the batsman's place, so much the better. Important things to study are: (1) the taking of overpitched balls by keeping down and taking them on the half-volley, without putting the legs together; and (2) the taking of leg-balls by moving the left leg sideways and a little forward, rather than sideways and backwards. This is most important.

Once again I would urge that the wicket-keeper's position should be flat-footed.

CHAPTER II

SUMMER NETS

THE nets can be of great value, or a source of weakness and deterioration. It all depends upon the quality of the wickets and how they are used. It is better to have no nets at all than to have nets with bumpy and dangerous pitches; these are useless for teaching batting and bowling, and may easily cause boys to draw away in natural and justifiable fear. Thus are bad habits developed; and they are difficult to cure. There is not much excuse for such wickets. A well-laid concrete pitch is not expensive, and pre-cast wickets can now be purchased. Here I must give a word of warning. The wicket must be laid on truly level ground. A perfect concrete wicket laid on a slight slope, with the batsman's end a little higher than the bowler's, will cause the balls to rise unnaturally high and vice versa. Coconut matting should be stretched tightly over the concrete, which should therefore be slightly smaller than the matting; this will enable the iron pins to be driven into the ground all round the wicket.

Let us suppose you have a really good turf or concrete net-wicket. How are you going to use it? Many of my readers are, no doubt, already experienced Cricket Masters having their own well-tried methods. All that I can do is to give my views in the hope that some points may be of interest and value.

I think that the first nets of the season should have as their object, enjoyment, a loosening of the muscles, and a re-discovery of the timing of a moving ball after the

Winter work in the gym. After a few such nets the serious work of teaching and practice can begin. If the boys have learned their strokes during the Winter they will know what they are *trying* to do. Experienced cricketers are apt to forget how little a boy knows even what he *wants* to do. If a boy does know this it is a big step, in fact a giant's stride, towards doing it. When a master sees a boy committing three or four different mistakes in the course of a few balls, it is very hard not to tell him of them all, which puts him into thorough confusion. Let one mistake be tackled at a time and much more rapid progress will result. Moreover, one fault cured will often obviate several others.

Nets are, in my opinion, for the batsman and the bowler. The system of leaving one side open so that other boys may get fielding practice is not a good one, as the attention of the coach is distracted from the real job in hand. Furthermore, the fielding practice is useless unless the fielders throw in hard, and there is danger and waste of time if they do so.

The bowlers should try to bowl the type of ball asked for by the master. It is a mistake to think that the bowling of long-hops to leg, if done intentionally and by order, will spoil a boy's bowling. If, at will, he can bowl half-volleys on the off or leg-balls he is learning control of length and direction; and he will probably be much better able to bowl good length straight balls when required. This will also help the batsman, as he can have a succession of similar balls of the type for which he needs practice.

The whole of the batsman's net should not be of this kind; but in a net of fifteen minutes, ten minutes should be used for such practice. During the last five minutes the bowlers should do their best to get his wicket, and he should imagine himself playing in a match. Never have

PLATE 15. This illustrates Points 1 to 4 and Point 10 of the first list in the bowling section of Part II and Points 1, 2, 3 and 5 of the second list. With such a good start the other Points would probably also have been correct. Look them up to see whether you agree!

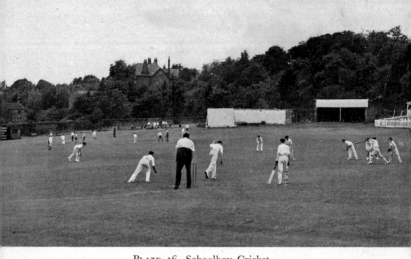

PLATE 16. Schoolboy Cricket

(*By permission of Westbourne Preparatory School, Ltd., Sheffield*)

PLATE 17. The Westbourne team snapped at the end of the Beech Hall match, of which a description is given. The names are as follows:

Seated, reading from left to right: Brown, Randles, Trott, Gardiner, Moncur, Jollie, Humberstone.

Standing: Wood, Cattell, Mr. R. G. Strutt, Woodhouse, de Dombal.

more than three bowlers per net, and let all three bowl before any ball is sent back.

FIELDING PRACTICES

Fielding practices are essential, and a routine should be followed to ensure that no department is missed. It is, of course, important that this should not lead to dullness. It can be avoided by introducing the competitive element. We have rounds of close, easy catches, close, hard catches, medium distance catches, long, high catches straight to the fielder, long, running catches followed by running in to the slow ball and flicking in underhand, stopping hard, straight ones, hard ones to right, hard ones to left, chasing the ball with *turning to the left* and throwing in. I generally give five points to each event; the weaker fielders thus gather a reasonable number of points from the easier catches. In the ground fielding I award one point for stopping the ball at all, one point for stopping it cleanly and three points for the throw. These three points are earned for length, straightness and velocity respectively. The boys keep their own scores. Sometimes the competition is an individual one, sometimes by "Houses", occasionally on a larger scale for house points, and once a year, for the Fielding Prize. Each boy then has five of each kind, in order to level out the luck as far as possible.

THE GAMES

The ordinary school games should vary in character as the season progresses, and monotony must be avoided at all costs. Most Prep. Boarding schools play every day,

whereas the Prep. Day school generally has to be content
with games on two or three days per week. Yet the general
standard of play is much the same. I suspect monotony
in the daily games at the boarding schools, though I am
aware that there are notable exceptions.

I have found it a good plan to start the season
with one or two games in which the available time is
divided up evenly, so that each batsman has ten or fifteen
minutes at the wicket regardless of the number of times he
gets out. To add interest and the element of winning or
losing, the total number of runs scored by each side is
divided by the total number of wickets, thus finding the
better average.

After a few such games "pick-ups" are arranged,
when play is of a more match-like character, though
instruction and exhortation are indulged in! Mid-season
is the time for house matches, boarders *v.* day-boys,
1st XI bowlers with oddments *v.* 1st XI batsmen with
oddments, and so on. End of term games are dealt with
in the next chapter.

HOME MATCHES

Home and away matches are discussed in separate
chapters, but there is one very important point which
applies to all matches, viz. the knowledge of the rules of a
one-day match. The number of masters in charge of teams
who do not understand the rule is quite astonishing, and
many potentially interesting games are ruined by the lack
of this understanding. At the risk of being wearisome to
the *cognoscenti* I am determined to make this matter
clear, and then, as an instance, I shall give an account of
a most thrilling match we played last Summer. This will,
I am sure, recapture your interest.

The rule is as follows: The side *leading* on the 1st innings cannot fail to win the match unless they are ALL OUT (or have declared) in the second innings, and have a smaller aggregate than the other side. Here are some examples:

	A XI	B XI
1st innings ...	72	75
2nd ,, ...	130 (for 1 wkt. dec.) or all out)	23 for 9 wkts.

B XI wins because it led on the 1st innings and was not all out in the 2nd innings.

	A XI	B XI
1st innings ...	72	71
2nd ,, ...	104 (either all out or declared)	106 (for any number of wkts.)

B XI wins as it has the better aggregate.

	A XI	B XI
1st innings ...	72	71
2nd ,, ...	41 (all out)	42 (for no wkts.)

A XI wins because it led on the 1st innings and B XI's aggregate was not greater.

N.B.—If a definite result has been obtained on the first innings *NO* circumstances in the second innings can cause the match to end in a draw or a tie.

What scores of times I have met with the following greeting from the master in charge of our opponents: "Decision on 1st innings, of course"; to which I reply, "Why not play the ordinary rule for one-day matches?" If I see on his face a look of blank bewilderment I give it up there and then, and agree to a 1st innings decision, but if I see glimmerings of questioning interest, I try to explain—sometimes successfully, often unsuccessfully. It

is, of course, vital that this question should be settled
before the match begins, as it seems to be in questionable
taste to have such a discussion after one's own side has
been led on the first innings! I have found, however, that
in cases where we have won on the first innings and there
is plenty of time left the opposing master often has a much
more open and receptive mind!

Fortunately, no such difficulties occur when we play
against Beech Hall, Macclesfield, for their Cricket Master
is a true cricketer. On May 25th, 1949, we had the most
thrilling game of the season with them—a game which
would have been so short and poor under the 1st innings
decision idea. The match was from 2 p.m. to 6 p.m., with
a tea interval of half an hour. Beech Hall batted first.

SCORES

1st Innings

BEECH HALL, MACCLESFIELD

Massiah b. Cattell	o
Wallace b. Gardiner ...	o
Goodwin not out	17
Cartmell b. Gardiner ...	2
Betts b. Gardiner	o
Smith b. Gardiner	1
Taylor b. Gardiner ...	4
Hancock c. Humberstone b. Gardiner	o
Jones c. Gardiner b. Brown	o
Templeton b. Brown ...	o
Johnson b. Moncur ...	1
Extras	9
Total	34

Bowling: Gardiner 6 for 7, Brown 2 for 6.

WESTBOURNE PREP. SCHOOL, SHEFFIELD

Gardiner c. Johnson b. Betts	1
Trott b. Cartmell	5
Brown b. Betts	1
Jollie b. Cartmell	2
de Dombal b. Cartmell ...	o
Moncur b. Cartmell ...	2
Woodhouse b. Hancock ...	3
Wood b. Betts	2
Humberstone c. and b. Hancock	o
Cattell not out ...	o
Randles st. Massiah b. Cartmell	o
Extras	5
Total	21

Bowling: Cartmell 4 for 7, Betts 3 for 4.

2nd Innings

BEECH HALL			WESTBOURNE		
Massiah b. Gardiner	...	1	Gardiner l.b.w. b. Cartmell		31
Wallace l.b.w. b. Moncur	...	8	Brown run out		5
Goodwin b. Brown ...	...	14	de Dombal l.b.w. b. Cartmell		3
Cartmell not out ...	...	24	Jollie not out		14
Betts c. Woodhouse b. Moncur		0	Randles c. Johnson b. Betts		17
Smith l.b.w. b. Brown	...	9	Moncur not out		0
Taylor b. Moncur ...	...	1	Woodhouse ⎱		
Hancock ⎫			Wood ⎟		
Jones ⎬ did not bat			Humberstone ⎬ did not bat		
Templeton ⎟			Cattell ⎟		
Johnson ⎭			Trott ⎰		
Extras ...	...	5	Extras ...	...	7
Total (for 6 wkts. dec.) ...		62	Total (for 4 wkts.)	...	77

Bowling: Moncur 3 for 15, Brown 2 for 8.

Bowling: Cartmell 2 for 35, Betts 1 for 25.

In the first innings our captain (Duncan Gardiner) found his form and a spot, and Beech Hall were all out for 34, the only resistance coming from Goodwin, their No. 3, who was not out 17. We therefore came out to bat in a confident manner, having expectations of a 9 or 10 wicket win. But Gardiner was not the only one to find a spot.

Beech Hall bowlers Cartmell and Betts bustled us out for 21. Thus under the beloved "1st innings decision, of course" rule the match would have been over before the tea interval, and we should have filled up the remaining time with the dreary and aimless "three-quarters of an hour's batting each side". How different was the real thing. Westbourne's hope was to dismiss Beech Hall cheaply and then go for the runs; but the Beech Hall boys had other views and refused to be dismissed cheaply, Cartmell and Goodwin putting up a particularly good defence.

H

When they had a lead of 50 the Beech Hall captain came out to declare, leaving us an hour to get the runs. I felt that this was over-generous and queried it with him. I found that he did not understand the rule properly, being under the impression that as the 2nd innings "counted" they would have to get us all out. I pointed out that unless we got *them* all out and topped their aggregate his side had won the match. They had lost only four wickets, so that this was virtually impossible. They had only to bat on for certain victory; but I told him that if he cared to declare at such a time as would give us a just possible chance to get the runs, we should appreciate it, and there might be a good finish. He agreed, and the Beech Hall innings continued until they had a total lead of 75 for the loss of 6 wickets; their skipper then declared, giving us 35 minutes to score the necessary 76 runs to win.

Our opening pair, Gardiner and Brown, by aggressive batting and by taking sharp singles, put on a quick 32 before Brown was run out. de Dombal was l.b.w. at 3 and our very small, very able and most determined Jollie appeared. Ten runs later Gardiner was also l.b.w., which caused my high hopes to sink. However, Jollie was batting soundly, and Randles, a left-hander, clouted a quick 13, with the result that in the penultimate over 9 runs were required with 10 balls to come. Randles hit another 4, leaving 9 balls from which to score 5 runs.

This seemed good enough, but when Randles failed to connect with the next two balls and was caught by Johnson off the last ball of the over, things were again tense. Five runs to get, six balls in which to get them with a new batsman arriving. Jollie faces Cartmell. Two good balls—no score. Off the third ball, to my horror, Jollie runs a single. The new batsman is defeated but unbowled by the fourth ball, and a merciful bye off the fifth brings Jollie to the right end again. Three runs needed off the last ball of the match! Cartmell bowls a ball on the leg stump, just short of a length. Jollie throws his right leg to the off, faces the bowler squarely and cracks a lovely boundary past square-leg. Result—Westbourne has won by six wickets; yet if Jollie had hit *to* square-leg instead of past him Beech Hall would have won by 13 runs.

Joyous Schoolboy cricket, indeed, and for their masters! Radiant Westbourne boys; slightly disappointed, but thrilled and ungrudgingly admiring, Beech Hall boys; the whole scene bathed in the light of true sportsmanship. "Decision on the first innings, of course" my foot! (See Plate XVII).

There is one form of Home Match which requires special mention—The Father's Match. This can be a most enjoyable fixture but it has its dangers. In some schools the Fathers seem able to turn out only poor or very much out-of-practice players. A lighthearted and amusing game results, with the boys generally the winners. But not so in Yorkshire. So far as is possible, the Fathers invited are the parents of the boys actually in the School XI or Reserves. These fathers generally seem to be good club players. For some years our Fathers' XI has been managed so ably by one of the parents that splendid games have been the result, but nevertheless, the dangers are there. Amongst these dangers I list the natural desire of the parent not to lose cricket standing in his son's eyes, the tendency to hit the ball harder than any schoolboy could hit it (with consequent danger to young hands and bodies) and the discouragement to young slow bowlers to pitch them up. In this last connection I remember a particular case. I had a goodish slow bowler who was inclined to pitch short. By the end of the season I had induced him to pitch a good length against the ordinary under-fourteen batsman. When bowling to one of the Fathers he was pitching this good Prep. School length; but the vast Father could and did reach him on the half-volley, cracking him for six after six. That is most harmful and discouraging to such a boy. It ought to be said that the above-mentioned parent was not captaining the Fathers' side that year.

During my headmastership of a London Prep. School, years ago, we had a form of Fathers' Match which I consider superior and free from these dangers. I took a couple of my own old bats and sawed off such of the edges as the bowlers had not removed, leaving the bat only about two inches wide. The Fathers used these, and they were encouraged to try their very best—except that fast (man's) bowling was not allowed. Some thrilling games resulted. The good batsmen still played good, very watchful innings; the ball still went sweetly off the middle, but owing to the considerable lightening of the bat, the hits were not too hard; the yahoo batsman soon departed, and the Father who wished to maintain his cricket reputation with his son had a good excuse if he was bowled! In my opinion it is better for the morale of the boys to play against Fathers who are going all out under a definite handicap than against Fathers on super-ficially equal terms. Unless the Fathers are exceptionally clever, the boys will soon spot their attempts to cover up intentionally missed catches, leg-balls, run-outs, etc.

Am I stating the obvious when I say that the home school should consider themselves the hosts in a social as well as cricketing sense? The visiting side may contain young cricketers playing in their first match; there are no supporters from their own school, and they should be clapped on coming out to bat by the boys who are watching the match as well as by the fielding inside. The watchers should also be taught to watch the match rather than to rag about, and to give applause impartially for good work in the field or at the crease. Of course, intense excitement and applause during such a crisis as the end of the Westbourne *v.* Beech Hall game is understandable and desirable.

If the younger boys can watch the match quietly for a couple of hours I think that is all that should be expected of them and further attendance be voluntary.

It is a charming custom for the School Captain and Vice-Captain, together with the master, to meet and greet the visiting team. At tea each boy of the home side should make himself personal host to one of the visitors.

CHAPTER III

AWAY MATCHES

WHAT enormous fun "away" matches are! To begin with it generally means missing the last morning period of school. How important one feels as one marches out of the classroom with apparent unconcern, but smugly noting, all the same, the gaze of the less fortunate ones still sitting at their desks. My own school away-match days go back to the two- and four-horse brake period, when we sometimes had to leave school as early as ten o'clock with a grand piece of veal and ham and egg pie in a bag. Alas, the motor-car and coach have altered all this, but I urge an early start. To bat too soon after a journey is asking for trouble.

I remember that, for several years in succession, I went down by car from London to Bradfield (a matter of some 60 miles I suppose) with the Incogs. to play against the school. It was always a rush to get there in time for the 11.30 start, and each year we lost two or three good wickets very cheaply. I cannot be sure of the reason for this, but an idea which suggests itself is that for a couple of hours objects have been flashing by at from 30 to 60 m.p.h. upon which we have not focussed our eyes. When we get to the wicket a single object flashes by at from 30 to 60 m.p.h. and still we do not focus!

It is a good plan to start the journey at least half an hour before strictly necessary. If it is convenient at the other end the boys can change and then spend some twenty minutes knocking a ball about and generally freeing their muscles. Sometimes they will start throwing high catches to one another. This should be frowned on,

for, even if no fingers are damaged, the boys' throwing in
the match will probably suffer. In cases where it is not
convenient for the team to arrive early, a stop should be
made as near to the destination as possible for the team to
have a good run round.

UMPIRING

I am afraid that we Prep. School masters are bad
umpires, but not wilfully so. I have never had reason to
suspect unfairness on the part of any master, but of
ignorance I have seen much. Even those of us who know
the rules are apt to make many mistakes, and this may
be accounted for by lack of practice. Do I hear loud
laughter and the almost indignant remark, "Why, I take
a cricket game nearly every day of the week the whole
Summer term!" My reply is that *that* is not umpiring.
When a master is taking a game his attention is rightly on
many things at once. He is teaching cricket. He must be
aware that the bowler is tiring, that the batsman lifted
his bat incorrectly, that cover-point was not on the move
as the ball was bowled, that square-leg had his hands in
his pockets, that extra-cover was backing up well, that
the non-striking batsman was not so doing, that mid-on
had moved from the position into which his captain had
placed him—and many other things all at once.

Real umpiring requires one's whole attention, and in
matches should get it, but there are probably only about
eleven or twelve matches in the whole term. In this connection it may be recalled that the decisions of the Australian
umpires during the first post-war tour of the M.C.C. came
in for much criticism by Australians themselves, but as an
explanation and defence, it was stated that they were not
in sufficiently good practice, owing to the scarcity of first-

class cricket during the war years. Frank Chester, perhaps the most famous of present-day umpires, states that he considers it just as important that umpires should have plenty of umpiring as that players should have plenty of practice. He adds that they should have good sight and hearing.

We cannot, therefore, expect to avoid a number of mistakes but, as a body, we can be a great deal better than we are. How? (a) By knowing the rules. Some masters do not yet know the new l.b.w. rule, and stand in such a position that they could not apply it if they did; (b) By real concentration during matches. (c) By knowing the signals. I have actually seen a master signal a boundary with the signal for a wide. (d) By calling "no ball" much quicker. McCanlis recently gave a very good tip on the subject in *The Cricketer*. He said that the umpire should time his respiration by the bowlers run-up so that he could yell "no-ball" that fraction of a second sooner which makes all the difference to the batsman. (e) By realizing our limitations and giving ourselves a little longer to weigh things up before giving a decision—even at the risk of being considered by others of being guilty of *in*decision.

It is most important that the exact hours of play should be settled before the match, and that the umpires should synchronize watches. Prep. School matches are carried on in the most delightful atmosphere of sportsmanship, but when there is a very tight finish, a difference of a couple of minutes between the umpires' time-pieces can be a source of embarrassment to both sides.

Above all, the master must resist the temptation, a terribly strong temptation, to which I must confess to have yielded occasionally, to give advice to his own side during the time he is umpiring. If the master sees quite plainly the way an obstinate batsman might be removed, it is very hard for him not to discuss the matter with the captain while waiting for the arrival of the new batsman at the other end. There seems to be no reason, however, why the master should not make suggestions at the tea interval.

Here is a point that is not generally known, viz. that there is no obligation on the part of the umpire to call "last over". It is not always possible since the rule has been changed, and is such that if there is time to start another over that over shall be finished. If overs have been taking about two and a half minutes and there are four minutes to go, it would obviously be wrong to call "last over"; yet in fact it may be the last over. Several boundaries may be scored involving long pilgrimages after the ball, or a batsman may sustain a temporary injury. That is no new problem; but the rule takes effect when, perhaps, three minutes remain for play. If the over then takes two and a half minutes, there is still time to start another one, and that over must be finished, even if a batsman gets out. The rule has certain qualifications, but I will leave the reader to study it himself. This will compel him to get a book of rules, which will be no bad thing. Naturally, if only one minute remains when an over starts it is quite in order to call it.

END OF TERM GAMES

Towards the end of term the character of the games may well be changed. The team bowlers and leading batsmen have had much cricket, probably considerable success, and though there may still be a match or two to come, can afford to take a back seat. If the lesser lights are allowed to bat early in the order, and to open the bowling, it gives them a thrill which stimulates their keenness. It is also a good policy; for the master can begin to think of next year's team and to note faults and weaknesses in individuals which can be tackled in the gym. during the Winter. Next year's probable opening pair can get accustomed to batting and running together; and can overcome, to a certain extent, stage-fright. The new bowlers get encouragement, as they no longer feel that they are being put on as a last hope. Hitherto they have probably never had a ball against batsmen who were not "set", and a wicket or two will help them to gain confidence.

GAMES WARDENS

Every "game" should have its own bag with a supply of the necessary sizes of bats, pads and gloves and a set of stumps and bails. For the last few years I have found it very helpful to appoint a couple of Games Wardens for each game. These boys are responsible for seeing that the right number of each article is in the bag at the end of the game, and for carrying away the bag. The boys generally take a keen interest in their job and enjoy the sense of responsibility. If Wardens are chosen outside the ranks of prefects and sub-prefects it is good training for them, and gives masters the opportunity of appraising their probable future usefulness in positions of greater responsibility. The Wardens should also bring to the notice of the master any minor repairs needed to the equipment before the damage gets serious.

With regard to the equipment itself I cannot too strongly urge the desirability of good quality. A boy should not be expected to bat with a dead lump of wood in his hands. If the bats vary in quality they soon find out the good ones, and are tempted to use them even if of unsuitable size. On this subject most masters will have discovered that it is impossible to buy good bats smaller than size three. Smaller than that the bats are atrocities which are merely toys, suitable for nothing but tennis-ball cricket on the sands.

Before the last war, I used to have well-proportioned bats, made specially for the very small boys from the age of five, with proper cane and rubber handles. This had to be given up during the war. As an expedient, I used to take old size three bats which had become damaged at the bottom or edges, and cut them down and shave them down into a semblance of proportion. It made the driving part rather near the bottom, but this was not always a disadvantage against the multiple bouncers encountered in Game 6! If the handle is also shortened, it does not require so very much to be taken off the bottom.

Balls *must* be good ones in spite of the present high prices. Cheap balls are much more hurtful to the hands and bodies of the youngsters, and also damage the bats. There is now available a very worthwhile economy. Certain firms and individuals, whose advertisements appear in *The Cricketer*, operate a cricket-ball renovation service. A ball in good condition, which has been used for only a single match, can be sent to such firms in the winter. For half a crown the ball is made to look like new and can be used for a match the next season. I had a number so treated last year and put them with my new balls. It was hard to tell "t'other from which".

Batting gloves are of the greatest importance, and the master should, in my opinion, insist upon their use during all games and nets. Boys frequently discard them, saying that they are uncomfortable. This is often due to the fact that they are of the wrong size. If the gloves are too tight or too sloppy a boy cannot be blamed for taking them off. It certainly is a problem, as the boys' hands vary so much in size and gloves are expensive. The modern fabric glove is much less adaptable than the type which has the thumb pad on a separate piece of elastic, for the elastic can be wound round the wrist a greater or less number of times. Also the elastic keeps the glove fingers well pulled down into place even if they are, strictly speaking, too large for the boy.

Pads are not such a severe problem, but they are soon apt to get worn by the boots. If they are repaired immediately they show signs of needing it, before any of the stuffing has come out, they will last for years. Small boys are very fond of crossing the straps at the knee; but this practice should be forbidden, as it throws a side or tearing strain on the stitching of the straps to the pads. Buckles should be worn on the outside of the legs and in cases where the boys own their own pads the unnecessary length can be cut off. In the case of communal pads, the straps must be left long enough for the fattest legs. The boys with thin legs must stow the unwanted ends as best they can, and they certainly should not be allowed to go in to bat with long ends flapping—as they certainly will unless they are instructed. Another common fault with small boys is that they do up the top strap tightly—a frequent cause of the stitching being torn.

STUMPS

The latest recommendation of the I.A.P.S. is that stumps should be of full size. I fully agree. The miniature sets one sometimes meets in Prep. School matches are an exasperation to the good boy bowler, when bowling to a "rabbit", as ball after ball passes an inch or two over the stumps. On the other hand the good boy batsman is quite capable of defending the larger stumps, and the "rabbit" must learn to bat.

CHAPTER IV

DISCUSSIONS AFTER WATCHING
COUNTY MATCHES

SOME advice was given in Part I as to how boys should take the fullest advantage of any opportunities of watching Test and County Cricket. Masters can help by reminding a boy to give craftsman's attention to the technique of the great exponents of that branch of cricket which he is studying in particular. But the master cannot be sitting next to more than two boys at a time, and his chief contribution to the educative side may well be the organizing and controlling of a discussion next day. Boys enjoy this; and they have often amazed me by the shrewdness of their comments which have shown the keenness of their observation. One such shrewd remark will help all the other members of the group, as well as provide the master with an opportunity to give a piece of instruction in an easy and profitable manner. He can also lead the discussion in any direction he wishes.

In my own opinion the greatest care should be taken not to discourage a boy's hero-worship. It would be far better for him to accept as perfect, and to emulate, a great player than to become an unimaginative critic. Yet great players sometimes have faults; and sometimes their apparent faults are really evidences of their greatness. The master who is striving to give a boy a true cricket education is faced with exactly the same problems as is the teacher of any subject of an artistic nature, and his success will depend largely upon his tact. The boy who has only recently taken any interest in reading and who is now thrilled by a Wild West story of poor literary quality will not be helped by a ruthless criticism of the book. Yet, at some stage, he must become aware of its faults and develop a true appreciation of literary masterpieces. The good teacher of English will lead him rightly, whereas the poor one will antagonize him. And so it is with cricket. The balance between hero-worship and informed criticism is a delicate one.

Last Summer we were watching a world-famous fielder in action. His speed of movement and clean picking up were a delight. His throwing action was perfection, but ball after ball was reaching the wicket-keeper at an awkward length. They were bad throws. Something had to be said. Such throws must not be considered as examples to be copied, though their velocity and straightness made a superficial appeal. Perhaps this fielder was a little careless that day; perhaps he had a touch of neuritis in his arm; perhaps some muscle in his back was strained. I feel sure that the badness of the throws ought not to be passed without comment; and I think that the last, rather than the first, possible reason should be suggested.

A great batsman may be retreating towards the square-leg umpire, and square-cutting good length, straight balls. The state of the game may warrant the risk, or perhaps he is enjoying one of those rare and miraculous days or periods when *any* stroke is not only possible but easy. Personally I have had three such experiences only in my cricketing life. Once it started suddenly and left me equally suddenly during the course of an otherwise normal innings; once after a laboriously compiled fifty; once from the first ball of my innings. The cause is obscure, but the fact that such things are possible explains many curious things one sees on the cricket field. The boys have been taught that it is bad batting to draw away to leg. They are now watching the great man doing this very thing. The matter cannot be ignored. It must be ventilated during the discussion. The educative possibilities of such discussions are endless, and are only limited by the matter of time.

CRICKET AS AN ART

I tackle this final section of my book with great trepidation. A plea for Cricket as an Art should only be made by a gifted writer; whereas I am merely a schoolmaster writing about cricket for boys. Nevertheless, so strong is my feeling on the subject that I cannot refrain from having a crack at it.

Cricket should be neither pure spectacle nor mere battle. Only one thing can be more dreary than big hitting against weak bowling, and that is negative bowling opposed by negative batting. Trench warfare should find no place on the cricket field; but this by no means excludes the splendour of stout defence against scintillating attack.

Cricket should be an opposition of skills and a contest of wills. Craftsmanship there should be; but this has an artistic beauty of its own only in so far as it contributes to the beauty of the whole. And what a whole it is! The Summer skies and fluttering flags, the green grass and yellow stumps, the clear but narrow creases marked out by the groundsman with geometrical neatness, the sea of faces round the ground and the great murmur as the umpires appear, the lithe and lovely movements of the white-clad young bowlers and fieldsmen, the mastery of the great opening batsmen, the tensity of the early overs of furious attack, and later, the gracefully curving balls from the slow bowlers concealing ophidian guile; sometimes the sustained crescendo of mounting anxiety; sometimes the sudden and dramatic reversal of the situation;

sometimes the nobly-masked weariness of the fielders towards the end of a long, hot day; sometimes the courageous indifference of the batsman to a cruel blow from a fast ball.

All this and much more is cricket.

Utility and "safety first" are alien to the game; but how can be found the balance between foolhardiness and aggression; between ultra-caution and stern defence? Only by absorbing the spirit of cricket and realizing it as an art. Appreciation of this, as of other arts, can be taught, or, I should prefer to say, imparted by a master to boys. Results may not immediately be apparent, but if he sows the seeds and cares for the young shoots there will be a lovely flowering in later life.

Rash flicking at rising off-side balls will rightly be discouraged; but the late cut should not be frowned upon because it is not a "safe" shot, nor should batsmen and spectators be denied the glory of the off-drive—through over-caution. Batsmen should try to win by making runs, and bowlers by taking wickets. The obtaining of a favourable result, on paper, by the use of negative methods is only one degree less reprehensible than the time-wasting crawl to the wicket of the in-going batsman when his side is striving to play out time.

The future of cricket will be in the hands of the present boys; but we masters can influence its destiny— now.

THE END